ADVANCED REVIEWS FOR
THE TAO OF ORDINARINESS: HUMILITY AND SIMPLICITY IN A NARCISSISTIC AGE

"In the chaos of our modern world Robert Wicks elucidates the concepts of humility, simplicity, courage and persistence as integral strategies to achieving inner peace. *The Tao of Ordinariness* provides a roadmap for achieving clarity and acceptance of the uniqueness of self as a pathway to contentment and resilience. This is a welcome recipe as many of us struggle with ambiguity, uncertainty and the pressures of modern life."

Patricia Davidson, Ph.D., M.Ed., RN, FAAN
Dean
Johns Hopkins School of Nursing

"So much energy is wasted on seeking to be someone or something we are not, but in this engaging and entertaining book Robert Wicks shows us the importance of being who we are. Bringing over forty years of clinical experience in helping others, and with wit and wisdom garnered from literature, philosophy, and psychology, this book is a great guide for everyone seeking to explore the possibilities within themselves."

Stephen Joseph, PhD.
Author, *Authentic: How to Be Yourself and Why It Matters*

"Learning to accept what life hands us may be our biggest challenge. *The Tao of Ordinariness* is a wise and timely reminder that being ordinary means living the truth of who we are by facing life just as it is."

Cheryl Giles, Psy.D.
Francis Greenwood Peabody Senior Lecturer on Pastoral Care and Counseling;
Core Faculty, Buddhist Ministry Initiative
Harvard Divinity School

"Robert Wicks takes us on an important journey; one of enlightenment and deep learning (and unlearning), if only we are open to listening, seeing, feeling, and experiencing what he shares with us. By peeling back the layers of interference from the world we have lived in and been influenced by, Wicks guides all those who seek the answers within. For all those who are open to embracing this process, this book opens the door to an important journey that can lead us to the happiness, contentment, and wholeness we each seek."

Jeffrey E. Barnett, Psy.D., ABPP
Past President, Psychotherapy Division, American Psychological Association;
Co-Editor, *Handbook of Private Practice* (Oxford University Press)

PRAISE FOR PREVIOUS RELATED BOOKS BY ROBERT J. WICKS

Night Call: Embracing Compassion and Hope in a Troubled World
(Oxford University Press: 2018)

"Robert Wicks, a renowned psychologist and specialist in the area of resilience, has written a truly impressive book."

Robert Brooks, Ph.D.,
Faculty, Harvard Medical School;
Co-author of *The Power of Resilience*

"With stories and words of wisdom, Wicks shows how persistence, compassion, and humility heal us all. His book is a great salve."

Robert F. Kennedy, Jr.
Perspective: The Calm within the Storm (Oxford University Press: 2014)

"This is the kind of book you can't put down because it is so necessary."

Alexandra Fuller
N.Y. Times Bestselling Author of Cocktail Hour under the Tree of Forgetfulness

Bounce: Living the Resilient Life
(Oxford University Press: 2010)

"Insightful, practical, and often humorous, *Bounce* is the right tonic for the spirit we need in a stressful world."

Helen Prejean
Author, *Dead Man Walking*

Riding the Dragon
(Sorin Books: 2003/2012)

"Like a good friend's support in tough times, *Riding the Dragon* is compassionate and wise."

Jack Kornfield
Author of *A Path with Heart*

Crossing the Desert: Learning to Let Go, See Clearly and Live Simply
(Sorin Books: 2017)

"*Crossing the Desert* offers the reader inspiration, insight, and invaluable tools for discovering the sacred presence in daily life."

Tara Brach
Author, *Radical Acceptance*

"Wonderfully sane, balanced, accessible, witty, and challenging."

Ronald Rolheiser
Author, *The Holy Longing*

The Tao of Ordinariness

Humility and Simplicity in a Narcissistic Age

ROBERT J. WICKS

Author
Night Call:
Embracing Compassion and Hope in a Troubled World

OXFORD
UNIVERSITY PRESS

OXFORD
UNIVERSITY PRESS

Oxford University Press is a department of the University of Oxford. It furthers
the University's objective of excellence in research, scholarship, and education
by publishing worldwide. Oxford is a registered trade mark of Oxford University
Press in the UK and certain other countries.

Published in the United States of America by Oxford University Press
198 Madison Avenue, New York, NY 10016, United States of America.

CIP data is on file at the Library of Congress
ISBN 978-0-19-093717-1

1 3 5 7 9 8 6 4 2

Wicks, R. (2010) *Bounce: Living the Resilient Life.* (New York: Oxford University Press).
Used with permission of Oxford University Press.
Thank you to Ave Maria Press for permission to reprint select excerpts from the following
books, all authored by Robert J. Wicks: *Availability: The Challenge and the Gift of Being Present;
Crossing the Desert; Streams of Contentment;* and *Touching the Holy.* 1-800-282-1865;
www.avemariapress.com.

Printed by Integrated Books International, United States of America

For my son-in-law, Peter Kulick. His simplicity and genuineness put others at ease. In being nothing less nor nothing more than who he is, he exemplifies the rare spirit of authenticity that marks the virtue of a truly "extra-ordinary" person. His example reminds me of what a gift it can be to those around us when we are simply ourselves. I know he is certainly a fine role model for me to emulate in this respect.

Thank you, Peter.

CONTENTS

Epigraph xi

INTRODUCTION: COMING HOME TO
YOURSELF *1*

~ GATEWAYS TO ORDINARINESS ~

ONE
AN ELUSIVE COMPANION
VIRTUE: HUMILITY *23*

TWO
TRAVEL LIGHTLY: SIMPLICITY AND
LETTING GO *53*

THREE
THE UNRECOGNIZABLE YOU: ADDRESSING THE
REPUTATION YOU CURRENTLY HAVE WITH
YOURSELF *80*

FOUR
BECOMING "SEA-KINDLY": LIVING WITH
GREATER PATIENCE, PERSEVERANCE, AND A
WILLINGNESS TO FAIL *112*

FIVE

MENTORS IN ORDINARINESS: EXPERIENCING
AUTHENTICITY IN PRACTICE   *138*

SIX

ALONETIME: EMBRACING SPACES CONDUCIVE
TO THE PROCESS OF SELF-UNCOVERING AND
RE-DISCOVERING   *164*

EPILOGUE: RETURNING HOME TO
YOURSELF . . . *AGAIN*   *185*

Notes   *203*

Sources Cited   *207*

About the Author   *213*

Index   *217*

If you are lost in the forest, that is not really lost.
You are really lost if you forget who you are.[1]
~AJAHN CHAH

The punishment imposed on us for claiming true self can never
be worse than the punishment we impose on ourselves by failing
to make that claim. And the converse is true as well: no reward
anyone might give us could possibly be greater than the reward that
comes from living by our own best lights.
~PARKER PALMER, *Let Your Life Speak*

When you start to live outside yourself, it's all dangerous.
~ERNEST HEMINGWAY, *Garden of Eden*

INTRODUCTION: COMING HOME TO YOURSELF

*So, as long as you are trying to be something other than what you
actually are, your mind merely wears itself out.*
—KRISHNAMURTI, *Life Ahead*

*I have often thought that the best way to define a man's character
would be to seek out the particular mental or moral attitude in
which, when it came upon him, he felt himself most deeply and
intensely active and alive. At such moments there is a voice inside
which speaks and says: "This is the real me!"*
—WILLIAM JAMES, Philosopher, and father of
American psychology

As an adult, simply being your own self can be surprisingly difficult. That is why people often pretend to be someone else. Yet, when we experience the lost virtue of "ordinariness" lived out by us or sense this freedom expressed in others, it can be truly amazing. American writer and naturalist, Henry Beston, wrote in his classic work *The Outermost House* that "no one really knows a bird until he has seen it in flight." I think the same can be said of us as persons when we are freely experiencing, being, and sharing ourselves.

Sometimes we can sense this when photographs capture vibrant passing moments in time—especially in the case of very young people. The photos let us participate in a spontaneous revelation of who the person was at that early juncture in life. In addition, they foretell of marvelous opportunities for the future *if* they are not totally lost.

In my own case, I immediately think of photographs of my two granddaughters when they were very young. One photo is of the older of the two, Kaitlyn, beaming with joy after unwrapping the gift of a toy doctor's kit. The other is of the younger one, Emily, dancing freely in a red turtleneck and fancy dress thrown on over it. She is holding up one arm, reaching for the sky, with a wondrous look of sheer joy on her face.

Seeing such favorite family photos even now helps me to appreciate more deeply the old practice of the wise Bantu tribesmen as they sought to guide their children toward greater fullness in life. They would slip into the rooms of their children when they were sleeping and whisper into their ears, "*Become what you are. Become what you are.*" However, the seeming magic of youthful exuberance, and the expression of such spontaneous "*extra*-ordinariness" as to who we are, is unfortunately easily undervalued, distorted, or even lost for many of us later in life.

And so recognizing this challenging reality and appropriately valuing the often now lost or forgotten virtue of ordinariness needs to be done with intention and determination. In the words of poet, e.e. cummings, "To be nobody but yourself in a world which is doing its best, night and day, to make you everybody else—means to fight the hardest battle which any human being can fight, and never stop fighting."

Fortunately, some of us occasionally do recognize the importance of discovering for ourselves the individuality and significance of ourselves and each person we meet—especially if that person is close to us. Sadly enough though, this may occur at a particularly poignant or tragic moment in our lives. When my wife had a miscarriage in the final trimester of her pregnancy, she taught me anew the importance of the uniqueness of every human being. When I asked her how she felt about losing the baby, she indicated that she was naturally quite sad about it, but there was one specific thing that particularly upset her. She said, "When I think of the son or daughter we have lost, the one point which tears me apart the most is that we shall never know who our child really was or would become. Would he have been a hyperactive boy? Would she have been a pensive girl? We will never know, and that holds a special sadness for me."

Yet even when the uniqueness of a person is welcomed for who that person is—not simply who or what we would want them to be—it still may not be straightforward. Recognizing and letting go of masks and flowing with one's natural and developed gifts and talents can be confusing. This is especially so at the beginning of the search for our simple, unvarnished ordinary selves. Not surprising then, this is one of the initial major goals of being in a therapeutic, coaching, or mentoring relationship, or when participating in some type of psychological or spiritual search. It is also the quest of this brief book on revisiting ordinariness and learning ways to come home to yourself in fresh ways.

Naturalist Peter Matthiessen immersed himself in such a search during a trek to find and photograph the elusive snow leopard in the Himalayas. During this period he was in the early stages of a Buddhist journey toward personal discovery and greater inner freedom. One of the reactions he reported in response to embarking on such an endeavor is not unusual. Psychological and spiritual journeys can (and, maybe, *must*) be disconcerting at times. In his book *Nine Headed Dragon* he relates, "It is difficult to adjust because I do not know who is adjusting; I am no longer the old person and not yet new." However, as he emphasized later in the book, the journey, even with its ups and downs, twists and turns, was worth it.

Fathoming our self—our *ordinary*, unvarnished self as it almost magically unfolds—is also a key part of the ongoing creative work of artists and poets. In this, they are great role models for all of us. In one of the passages in *Letters to a Young Poet*, Rilke advises his junior correspondent—and us today—by writing:

> If your daily life seems poor, do not blame it; blame yourself, tell yourself that you are not poet enough to call forth its riches; for to the creator there is no poverty and no poor indifferent place. And even if you were in some prison the walls of which let none of the sounds of the world come to your senses—would you not then still have your childhood, that precious kingly possession, that treasure house of memories?

Turn your attention thither. Try to raise the submerged sensations of that simple past; your personality will grow firm, your solitude will widen and will become a dusky dwelling past which the noise of others goes by far away.

Still, extolling the value of being our ordinary selves is one thing. Seeing how this can become possible is obviously quite another matter. Sarah Bakewell, in her delightful work *At the Existentialist Café*, notes that the writer and philosopher Iris Murdoch "observed that we need not expect moral philosophers to 'live by' their ideas in a simplistic way, as if they were following a set of rules. But we can expect them to show how their ideas are lived *in*. We should be able to look in through the windows of a philosophy, as it were, and see how people occupy it, how they move about and how they conduct themselves." The same can be said with respect to ordinariness. In the same breath that we speak of the value of being truly ourselves, we must also appreciate and be open to particularly helpful routes to uncover who we might be and live out of this awareness *now* in an authentic way. Accomplishing this—especially in today's world—takes both intention and knowledge as to how best to value and return to who we simply are as people.

Studying and embracing ordinariness is like taking an unself-conscious inner journey. The goal is not to reinvent ourselves into someone who we innately are not. It is to embrace the heart of our talents and face our foibles and growing edges without recrimination for who we are not nor may ever be. Such an inner journey also includes undertaking a psychological pil-grimage to the different parts of ourselves that haven't yet fully seen the light of day. This is done so that, once acknowledged, they can be claimed. After all, we can't take responsibility for an emerging fuller sense of self if we don't know it exists.

To accomplish such a sense of greater personal awareness, it is important that emotional "space" and a nonjudgmental attitude be present so the sense of self can be fathomed more clearly, completely, and forthrightly. One of the times this nat-urally happens is during adolescence. It is especially during this time that persons usually play with possibilities as a way of exploring aspects of self. This is often attempted by viewing and acting out reflections of others that are deemed "prob-able." The passion of this sometimes tumultuous stage ideally gives way to the true claiming of "ordinary me," which, to be honest, is hard work because of all the outside influences that are present. Given the fearful forces that surround many young people, the choices taken at this point often unfortunately wind up being "masks" that are acceptable to those around them. Eventual submission to the values of "the other" often seems easier, even though it is usually less satisfying in the long run. In fact, it can be deadly to the fulfillment of a dream embraced in early years—namely, the greater understanding, prizing, and flowering of who we are and able to become—a process society often plays down or resists.

Roger Housden, in his book *Ten Poems to Change Your Life*, serves to underscore this when he cautions, "Whatever your circumstances, people will start to give you advice as soon as you disturb the status quo. That advice is likely to be bad. It will be bad because they are seeking, not to understand further your calling, but to preserve the world as they know it."

His point is echoed from the following vantage point by Stephen Joseph, in his book *Authentic: How to Be Yourself and Why It Matters*:

> Authentic people will not try to control or manipulate others. They respect others' right to be the agents of their own life, because that is what they expect for themselves from others. When faced with attempts to control or manipulate them, authentic people resist external pressures to go along with how others think. They will not conform to ideas, opinions or views because others want them to, or because that is the majority view. They will weigh up evidence for and against an argument, reach their own judgement and hold their ground on what they think rather than compromise themselves.

Today, being ordinary is to act in a countercultural fashion. In a world now clearly mesmerized by "spin," narcissism, exhibitionism, and image-making, the material that follows centers on revisiting a virtue seemingly set aside by contemporary society. The fact that psychology and the classic wisdom literature have long valued being ordinary is drowned out by many other voices that emphasize publicity over authenticity and humility. Many years ago, when author Flannery O'Connor was complimented by a friend on the publication of her book *A Good Man Is Hard to*

Find, she wrote back offering the warning that fame was merely "a comic distinction shared with Roy Rogers' horse and Miss Watermelon 1955." Today, in many cases her voice would fall on deaf ears.

The psychological paradox (more recently reflected in both positive psychology and narrative therapy) that will be presented in this book—and is designed to counteract dysfunctional current mores—is that once you accept your limits (a key aspect of ordinariness), the opportunity for growth and depth will seem almost limitless. Prior to that, much energy is wasted on seeking to be someone or something we are not as persons in order to attract and please the (often imaginary) crowd around us. One's existence in this case is spent in front of a virtual mirror, instead of leaving the stage to simply, and hopefully, live out in reality one's own life in the company of others who wish to do the same.

Austrian-born Jewish philosopher Martin Buber pointed to the call to be ordinary in a way that echoes a Christian spiritual theme referred to as *imago Dei* (being made in the image and likeness of God). It was presented as a recognition uttered by the Rabbi Zusya many years ago, in the following simple, powerful way:

"In the world to come I shall not be asked, 'Why were you not Moses?'

Instead, I shall be asked, 'Why were you not Zusya?'"

The thesis of *The Tao of Ordinariness* is that by walking through such psychological, philosophical, and spiritual portals as humility, simplicity, self-respect, "alonetime," *kenosis*, courage, perseverance, mentorship, and relationship, ordinariness can be revisited from a number of different vantage points to open it up in a new, welcoming fashion. The goal in doing this will be to foster the increase in a gentle clarity about one's own uniqueness that, once attained, can offer an encouraging space to others to appreciate their own sense of self as well.

For example, in Chapter I, on humility, one way of viewing ordinariness through the eyes of this other, elusive virtue will be discussed through exploration of the following thesis:

When you take knowledge and you add humility, you get wisdom.

Then, when you take this very wisdom and add it to compassion, you get love.

And love is at the heart of a rewarding and compassionate life.

And so the promise of *The Tao of Ordinariness* is essentially quite simple. It can also be far-reaching depending on how it is viewed and subsequently embraced anew. To encourage a reconsidering of ordinariness, the following chapters suggest ideas and direction to encourage each person to explore his or her own unique life for what it might—not what others say it *must*—be. It is also to help others—through our modeling of it—to do the same.

In an interview for *Mindful* magazine in June 2017, author Anne LaMotte, in her usual delightful, honest, and insightful way, indicated that she spent a great deal of time with children and noticed that she became "merciful and open when they are around. They're crazily generous. My grandson will give stuff away that I don't want him to give away. The merciful heart is really rich at four or five, but then it begins to diminish."

She then added a hopeful—and I believe realistic—note later in the interview:

> We come into the world merciful, and we can be that way again once we realize we have so many stories about ourselves and other people and so many defenses against feeling exposed. Little by little, we can start dropping that armor and practice being real instead of putting on those great social personas we've mastered. When you're real with somebody, they will be real back. And when you're back in your original, merciful, authentic selves, that breeds wonder and a deep sense of presence.

The impact expected in addressing the virtue of ordinariness is nothing less than moving one's life from merely involving daily efforts and skirmishes to protect, project, or build up one's image, to an approach that is more like a journey or pilgrimage in fullness and inner freedom. Moreover, as just indicated, enhancing ordinariness also results in offering "interpersonal space" to others so they can feel a similar freedom to accept and become more themselves as well. Examples of this can sometimes be seen in some family members, friends, acquaintances, or in such well-known persons as the Dalai Lama or Archbishop Desmond Tutu.

Once when Archbishop Tutu was speaking to a group of seminarians at General Theological Seminary in New York City, one of the seminarians in the audience nudged the dean who was sitting next to him. When the dean looked over at him, he whispered, "Desmond Tutu is a holy man." In response, when the dean asked him how he knew this, he didn't blink an eye but immediately said, "I know that Desmond Tutu is holy because when I am with him, *I* feel holy."

Most people have not only had such experiences with other "ordinary" people but also received similar feedback at times when they were "simply" themselves. In my own case, I remember once delivering a presentation to a packed room of 900 people at a large conference attracting over 20,000 participants. After delivering the presentation, a girl who appeared to be in her late teens or early twenties patiently waited in a line of people, most of whom had questions about what I had shared. When her turn came, instead of asking further clarification about something I had mentioned in my talk, she said, "Your presentation wasn't what I expected." Then, while I was starting to absorb this comment, she added, "Somehow, I thought you would talk down to us. Instead, you spoke about yourself, shared stories and ideas. You walked *with* us."

I was moved by her words more than those of any of the other people present. I knew, at least in this instance, that ordinariness and transparency, as well as my faith in those listening to my words (rather than simply expecting them to have trust in me), had come across. My own voice, which I tried to offer in a clear, honest, and direct way, seemed to have encouraged, in at least this one other person, a "space" in which to better find hers.

To move in this direction more often, we can practice some simple attitudes and tasks in seeking to find or expand our own voice. Core among them is the need to affirm that each person—including ourselves— has a unique style and gift worthy of being discovered and heard. Advertising, as a way of selling something, and society as a way of protecting a structure or value, may seek to prevent, destroy, or minimize this belief. However, as we have just seen, looking around at people who seem to be flowing with their lives and at ease with who they are, we find that ordinariness is something worthy to seek and value.

Financial status or education does not determine the happiness that comes with exploring and experiencing ease with ourselves. Nor do such things lead to possessing the freedom to let others be who they are. This is in sharp contrast to what others claim are requirements for satisfaction. Psychology and classic spirituality illustrate this in creative ways.

In his challenging and informative little book, *The Trauma of Everyday Life*, Buddhist psychiatrist Mark Epstein presents this wisdom in the following light:

A friend of mine who spent years in India with a great teacher from the ancient forest tradition tells a moving story

that, to my mind, makes the same point. Years after his beloved teacher had died, he was back in India staying at the
home of his guru's most devoted Indian disciple.

"I must show you something," the disciple said to my
friend one day. "This is what he left for me." My friend was
excited, of course. Any trace of his teacher was nectar to him.
He watched as the elderly man opened the creaking door of
an ancient wooden wardrobe and took something from the
back of the bottom of the shelf. It was wrapped in an old
dirty cloth.

"Do you see?" he asked my friend.

"No. See what?"

The disciple unwrapped the object, revealing an old,
beat-up aluminum pot, the kind of ordinary pot one sees in
every Indian kitchen. Looking deeply into my friend's eyes,
he told him, "He left this for me when he went away. Do you
see? Do you see?"

"No, Dada," he replied. I don't see."

According to my friend, Dada looked at him even more
intensely, this time with a mad glint in his eyes.

"You don't have to shine," he said. "*You don't have to shine.*"
He rewrapped the pot and put it back on the bottom shelf of
the wardrobe.

My friend had received the most important teaching,
one that had its origins in the Buddha's revolutionary approach. He did not have to transform himself in the way
he imagined: He just had to learn to be kind to himself.

If he could hold himself with the care Dada showed while clutching the old pot, it would be enough. His ordinary self, wrapped in all of its primitive agony, was precious too.

To arrive at such an insight, though, as in the case of the person in this story, we must be willing to take honoring ordinariness to heart by:

- Seeing the value of learning about and sounding like ourselves more and more.
- Affirming the belief that each person has a unique voice to be discovered through reflection, discussion with friends, and focusing on the talents and fears or training that hold them back from being enhanced.
- Taking risks that explore potential gifts we may not feel we have but which others have noted that they see in us.
- Honoring the discipline and patience that build on the courage to experiment with new behavior.
- Enjoying the process of observing ourselves as well as experimenting with fresh ideas and innovative behavior.
- Expanding our tolerance for failure and looking foolish because it comes with the fathoming of ourselves and our talents, as well as our unnecessary fears and anxiety. (After all, it is silly to grimly hold onto the side of the pool when we could swim in the ocean with a smile on our face.)

Having noted these actions, there is still a caveat worth mentioning: Knowing the way to accomplish the efforts just listed is not a *complete* prerequisite for discovering and enjoying being our ordinary self. There is still always a balance between mystery and effort in discovering, valuing, and sharing our sense of self.

Pat Schneider, in her book *Writing Alone and With Others*, writes about the search for her unique voice by admitting, "I feel tangled as if I am on the edge of a jungle and have lost my machete." The process of exploring what it means to "simply" be our ordinary self doesn't exclude a sense of being lost at times. Mystery is part of the search. Fear is as well. Part of the adventure of being ourselves in front of others—whether in actuality or in imagination—can be quite challenging. Yet, as well-known author and contemplative guide Thomas Merton, in his book *A Vow of Conversation* notes, such tough realities need not be the final extreme negative experience that holds us back: "What matters is the struggle to make the right adjustment in my own life and this upsets me because there *is no pattern* for me to follow . . . in freedom. Hence my fear and my guilt, my indecisions, my hesitations, my back tracking, my attempts to cover myself when wrong, etc." Yet, later he adds the following important addendum: The "answers tend to be confusing and to hide the truth for which one must struggle in loneliness—but why in desperation? This is not necessary."

The courageous people who came before us taught important lessons about ordinariness. In their struggles, they offered us models of the need to strive with all our might to be ourselves. In the words of the well-known inventor and global citizen, R. Buckminster Fuller,

> The only important thing about me is that I am an average, healthy human being. All the things I've been able to do, any human being, or any one, or you, could do equally well or better. I was able to accomplish what I did by refusing to be hooked on a game of life that had nothing to do with the way the universe was going. I was just a throw-away who was willing to commit myself to what needed to be done.

In line with both Merton's and Fuller's comments, in the quest to embrace ordinariness, we are not seeking another world for ourselves but the evolution of our own self within the world community. This, rather than a see-saw experience of denial and fantasy, is the very thrill and challenge of life, *our* life.

Mathematical genius Albert Einstein said, "He who can no longer pause to wonder and stand rapt in awe is as good as dead." This point is valid to no greater degree than in appreciating the loveliness of our uniqueness when we respond to what life, rather than society or advertising, is calling us to *be*.

We who live, have been born, and have a personality that can be known by us and honestly shared with others have a duty to encourage it to evolve. If we don't seek to allow it to blossom but instead abort or twist our talents to suit others, we actually mock existence and our singular place in it. In fact, the very community that may be causing us to adjust to its desires paradoxically will be lessened by the absence of our ordinary presence.

To fully develop we need an appreciation of our inherent value. We also need, to a greater degree, a recognition of our natural resistance to continue on the path toward freedom and health. American Jungian analyst John Sanford, in his book *Healing and Wholeness*, notes that even when we believe in the value of the continuing search for ways to develop, the process—as both Matthiessen and Merton also recognized—can be a discouraging battle. In the words of Sanford:

> Deep inside each organism is something that knows what that organism's true nature and life goal is. It is as though there is within each person an inner center that knows what constitutes health. If our conscious personality becomes related to the inner center, the whole person may begin to emerge, though this may not bring either peace or social adaptation, but conflict and stress. . . . The movement toward health may look more like a crucifixion than adaptation or peace of mind.

The struggle to help the whole person emerge requires a strong belief in the importance of not turning away from the truth about ourselves. The relief gained in putting up our defenses and avoiding who we are is only a temporary one. The trade-off for ignorance is too great, for in not fighting the good fight to be ourselves, as e. e. cummings urges, we die a bit each day, torn by our anxieties and compulsions, which keep us troubled, bored, and unsatisfied. We may, in fact, put others at ease who want us to conform, but we will never satisfy the restlessness or hunger for experiencing and living the life we feel we were called to live.

The Tao of Ordinariness seeks to take to heart the importance of seeing ourselves clearly, nonjudgmentally, in spite of the pressures to be someone or something else. By looking through different relevant thematic windows to appreciate ordinariness from varied vantage points, this book encourages a greater awareness and appreciation of it. This search is in line with the following wisdom from the East, reflected in some form in many sayings:

> Some dreamed of becoming somebody else in the eyes of others and merely existed.
>
> Others became more fully awake to who they really are . . . and became *alive.*

Such a goal is obviously a worthy one. What is not obvious is that rather than bravado, which is so often encouraged in contemporary society by those leading it, embracing ordinariness will require two other "softer" virtues not spoken about much today—*humility* and *simplicity.* These would seem to be two appropriate gateways to initially pass through in the search for a greater appreciation of ordinariness. In reviewing them we may find ourselves with thoughts similar to the following ones shared by David Brooks in the opening of his book, *The Road to Character:*

Recently I've been thinking about the difference between the résumé virtues and the eulogy virtues. The résumé virtues are the ones you list on your résumé, the skills that you bring to the job market and that contribute to external success. The eulogy virtues are deeper. They're the virtues that get talked about at your funeral, the ones that exist at the core of your being—whether you are kind, brave, honest, or faithful; what kind of relationships you have formed.

I think ordinariness, and related and supporting traits such as humility and simplicity, actually count among the eulogy virtues Brooks is speaking about. Thus the aim of this book is to bring these virtues more clearly into focus so they have a chance to take greater prominence in our lives at a time in society when this seems so crucial to its development.

~ Gateways to Ordinariness ~

Ordinariness is an attitude or stance that allows persons to explore and be intrigued by current realities and possibilities within themselves. It is marked by a comfort with oneself that leads to appropriate transparency. Essential aspects of enhancing the understanding and expression of personal ordinariness also include the courage to confront unhelpful external influences (even by those who purport to have one's best interests at heart); the true humility to honor one's talents while clearly and gently viewing shortcomings in an honest, nonjudgmental fashion; and a willingness to embrace and model a lack of egoism in one's interpersonal relations in ways that would encourage personal freedom in others and thus to become more fully themselves as well.

ONE

An Elusive Companion
Virtue: Humility

*The cup which has held garlic juice keeps the smell even though it
is cleaned and scoured hundreds of times. So the odor of egoism
never completely leaves us.*
—RAMAKRISHNA

*When you have ears to hear a bird in song, you don't need to look
at its credentials.*
—ANTHONY DE MELLO, *One Minute Wisdom*

In a delightful Jewish tale, a rabbi walks up to the front of
his almost empty synagogue, looks up to the heavens, raises
his arms in prayer, and loudly exclaims, "I am nothing. I am
nothing."

Seeing this, the cantor who was also present, walks up after
him and does the same—this time saying it with even more emphasis with his baritone timbre, "I am *nothing*. I am *nothing*."

A janitor standing in the rear of the synagogue was moved
by their example. And so, when they walked to the side to
confer on something, he also walked to the front of the synagogue. Then, like they did, he reached his arms toward the

heavens and prayed, "I am nothing. I am nothing." Seeing this, the rabbi turned to the cantor and said, "*Nu*, look who thinks he's nothing."

Humility has always been a very elusive virtue. It is impossible to seek it directly. To make matters worse, like its close relative, ordinariness, it also no longer seems valued or desirable in much of contemporary society. Today, especially in the public eye, it is not only ignored, it is shunned. At football games, unlike in the past when players got visibly excited—almost in a surprised way—when a play went well, now they often seem to go out of their way to seek and show an expectation for adulation from the crowd.

Yet, thankfully, some sports luminaries, even today, still demonstrate humility and prove you don't need to be exhibitionistic and self-centered when stardom touches your life. One example of this is Katie Ledecky, who is arguably one of the greatest—and certainly most decorated—swimmers of our time. This sense of modesty was shown at a Pro Series meeting when the then twenty-year-old multi–gold medalist took the time to introduce and praise a seventy-three-year-old gold medalist, Chris Olmsted, who came before her and had achieved so much. About this honoring of another amidst one's own period of achievement, sportswriter Karen Crouse wrote that the fact that she did this

> tells you more about Ledecky than she will ever volunteer. It's
> easy for today's celebrated sports figures to forget (or never

trouble themselves to know) that luminous stars existed long before ESPN [cable TV] came along and trained its magnifying lens on the sports constellation.

Ledecky is an exception, an enthusiastic student of swimming who recognizes her place on the sport's continuum better than those who are quick to consecrate her. When Olmstead sent an admiring email to Ledecky in January 2016, it was *the beginning of a friendship that has enriched them both.*

Few people know better than Olmstead, who competed as Chris von Saltza, what it is like to navigate one's teenage years as swimming royalty. Their shared bond has bridged their generation gap: Olmstead is 73, and Ledecky is 20. Through Olmstead, Ledecky has gained a deeper appreciation for all the opportunities that today's female athletes take for granted.

Such a model of ordinariness by an "extra-ordinary" young swimmer is an inspiration to all of us. The pre-teen fans present that day were taught by the example of one of their heroes that honoring others' skills is part of taking your own place in history. Whereas involving yourself in self-praise and unduly drawing attention to yourself is truly a narcissistic exercise that reveals your own insecurity and lack of respect for those upon whose shoulders you stand—no matter what your own accomplishments may be.

In politics, especially of late, it has become the same in certain quarters. During the 2016 U.S. presidential elections, a neighbor, who had observed many, many campaigns, told me she was upset by the choices she had. She was shocked by what one of the candidates had done. Not knowing exactly what she was referring to, I asked, "What did the candidate do?" She responded, "He walked out in front of the crowd and said, 'Am I not handsome? Am I not really good looking?'" You could tell by the expression on her face that this was something she had never experienced among leading candidates for political office in her over eighty years on this earth. At the time, I remember mumbling something to the effect that times had certainly changed, to which she responded with emphasis, "And not for the *better*, either!"

Shortly after that encounter I read an August 26, 2016, article, "The Art of Gracious Leadership," by *New York Times* conservative columnist, David Brooks, in which he reflected on the style of both presidential candidates:

> Lately I've been thinking about experience. Donald Trump lacks political experience, and the ineptitude caused by his inexperience is evident every day. On the other hand, Hillary Clinton is nothing if not experienced. Her ship is running smoothly, and yet as her reaction to the email scandal shows once again, there's a whiff of inhumanity about her campaign that inspires distrust.
>
> So I've been thinking that it's not enough to be experienced. The people in public life we really admire turn experience into graciousness.
>
> These people, I think, see their years as humbling agents. They see that, more often than not, the events in our lives are

perfectly designed to lay bare our chronic weaknesses and expose some great whopping new ones.

Sooner or later life teaches you that you're not the center of the universe, nor quite as talented or good as you thought. It teaches you to care less about what others think and, less self-conscious, to get out of your own way.

Months following Brooks' article, a more strongly worded opinion piece on religion and politics, "The Quiet Power of Humility," was published in the Sunday *New York Times* by Peter Wehner, a senior fellow at the Ethics and Public Policy Center who also served in the previous three Republican administrations prior to the Trump one.

He began this piece, which also reflected on the election of Donald Trump as president, by relating a key aspect of a conversation he had had with a social psychologist who, while an atheist, saw much to admire in religion. Wehner asked him "what constructive contribution Christians could make to public life." To this, the psychologist responded, "humility."

Wehner then went on to say that from his vantage point "humility is hardly a hallmark of American Christianity; especially (but by no means exclusively) among those Christians involved in politics." He then clearly pointed out the irony, once again in his words, that "prominent Christian leaders and a record number of self-proclaimed evangelical voters supported for president a man of undisguised cruelty and unmatched narcissism."

He closed his piece on a hopeful note and a calling that I think he was directing to all of us—not simply Christians or religious persons interested in politics—with the following words:

> A friend of mine recently told me that humility—a virtue he would be the first to admit he recognized only later in life—is elusive, a perpetual goal, almost a little bit out of reach. The wiser we become, the more we see how much we don't know and how much we need others to help us know.
>
> The greatest among you shall be a servant, Jesus said, and whoever humbles himself shall be exalted. For people of the Christian faith, no one humbled himself as much as Jesus himself. The cross made the resurrection possible; humility prepared the way for hope. Which raises this question: If humility was good enough for Jesus, why not for the rest of us?

As I reflect on these articles and my own experiences of the Trump candidacy and early days of his presidency, the most moving moment for me was *not* when Trump touted his accomplishments or indicated he was a "stable genius" but when he shared his vulnerability. In discussing his brother Freddy, who was reportedly an alcoholic and died at age forty-three, Donald Trump shared his love for his brother and sadness at his early passing. This moment of ordinariness, exemplified by personal vulnerability—whether he saw it as that or not—was to me the greatest moment of character strength demonstrated by him. It's sad that he didn't realize it, just as others like him in politics and some leaders or well-known and well-heeled television preachers fail to do. Even during those moments when the president was in situations where people were suffering, according to a report in the *Washington Post*, he consciously or without being aware of it seemed to come across as being more self-referential than being a healing presence. In the words of reporter Jenna Johnson:

> As rescuers continued their exhausting and heartbreaking work in southeastern Texas on Tuesday afternoon, as the rain continued to fall and a reservoir near Houston spilled over, President Trump grabbed a microphone to address hundreds of supporters who had gathered outside a firehouse near Corpus Christi, Texas and were chanting: "USA, USA, USA!"
>
> "Thank you, everybody," the president said, sporting one of the white "USA" caps that are being sold on his campaign website for $40. "I just want to say: We love you. You are special. . . . What a crowd. What a turnout"
>
> Yet again, Trump managed to turn attention on himself. His responses to the devastation caused by Hurricane Harvey have been more focused on the power of the storm and his administration's response than on the millions of Texans whose lives have been dramatically altered by the floodwaters.

In this article, Matt Latimer, who was a speechwriter for President George W. Bush, is quoted as acknowledging that it is a difficult balancing act for presidents when they address audiences after a natural disaster. However, he then adds, "You want to project confidence that things will get better, but at the same time you want to display empathy for people who have lost everything. . . . The president has a knack for the first one, but so far he hasn't displayed a lot of skill at displaying empathy. And that's a problem." Such a problem, albeit possibly to a lesser degree for many of us, is to use other's lack of empathy as a psychological mirror on ourselves.

One of the benefits for me in observing such events and others' lack of sensitivity to persons suffering because of the need for acceptance—and even adulation—is that it helps me come to my senses when wrapped in my own personal experiences and exhibitions of egoism. In such instances, I am also helped to recall the temptations to typecast people like Trump or others in ways that prevent me from seeing their gifts.

As Parker Palmer notes in his book, *Let Your Life Speak*, we must be able to bring everything home to ourselves so we can clearly embrace both our gifts and shortcomings. This is necessary, as he points out in the following quote, in the search for "wholeness" or what I would term "ordinariness".

> But if I am to let my life speak things I want to hear, things I would gladly tell others, I must also let it speak things I do not want to hear and would never tell anyone else! My life is not only about my strengths and virtues; it is also about my liabilities and my limits, my trespasses and my shadow. An inevitable though often ignored dimension of the quest for "wholeness" is that we must embrace what we dislike or find

shameful about ourselves as well as what we are confident and proud of.

However, this is very difficult for those personalities that are psychologically classified as being character disordered. For them it is always the "other" that is at fault. Nowhere in this category is this more pronounced than among what has been termed psychopaths or antisocial disorders. In her work, *Glass Houses*, novelist Louise Penny, whose works of fiction contain quite incisive psychological insights and descriptions, describes the problem with these individuals well—not only for them but also for those surrounding and impacted by them. This is illustrated next in a dialogue between Myrna, a retired psychologist, and Armand, the Chief Superintendent of the Sureté (Police Department):

> "You see that's the problem," said Myrna. "We're used to the film versions of psychopaths. The clearly crazies. But most psychopaths are clever. They have to be. They know how to mimic human behavior. How to pretend to care, while not actually feeling anything except perhaps rage and an overwhelming and near perpetual sense of entitlement. That they have been wronged. They get what they want mostly through manipulation. Most don't have to resort to violence."
>
> "We all use manipulation," said Armand. "We might not see it that way, but we do." . . .
>
> "Unlike most of us, who tend to be transparent, people rarely see through a psychopath," she continued. "He's

masterful. People trust and believe him. Even like him. It's his great skill. Convincing people that his point of view is legitimate and right, often when all the evidence points in the other direction. Like Iago. It's a kind of magic."

What makes matters worse for such individuals are the enablers around them. When such persons manipulate or rage rather than look at possible flaws in their own personality, thinking, or action, they are sometimes protected by those around them. Sometimes the defense is that "you don't know the real person" or "he or she only behaves this way in response to being attacked." In such cases, it may be obvious to almost everyone else around, but the defenders either don't see it or realize that they will be raged against if they even hint that the fault may lie with the antisocial characters themselves. I think most of us have experienced this either in our own interpersonal circle or on the larger stage.

But humility is a broader issue in the public arena beyond persons who resist insight in the areas of politics and religion— at least here in America. I could see this easily during an interaction with a visitor from another country. We spent some leisurely moments just passing the day, conversing about several things that struck him as a person from abroad. Finally, he stopped for a bit and then went on, "You know, I was looking through one of your daily newspapers and one in the United Kingdom online and I saw prominent coverage of a woman I had never heard of before." He then mentioned the name and

I recognized her as being part of a family that was frequently mentioned in the newspapers and online. They were portrayed always in ways that might be termed "exhibitionistic"; clearly, she and other members of her family sought and thrived on being in the limelight and the press—even if the story was a derogatory one.

He then asked, "Is she an actress, writer, dancer, or is she talented in some specific way?" When I responded, "No. She is simply famous," he looked as puzzled as I felt when I first saw her and her family featured again and again in the news for what they had said or how they had acted or the outfits they wore. Humility had no place to play in their ethos.

To make matters even more confusing today with respect to the virtue of humility is the recent distorted use of the concept and word *humble* by some on the public stage. Carina Chocano, the author of a book of essays, *You Play the Girl*, wrote in a *New York Times Magazine* (January 29, 2017) article, "Lying Low," that "being 'humbled' used to involve feeling diminished and unworthy. But lately, we've made it another expression of everyone's favorite subject: how great we are." She went on to say,

We are living in humbling times. People are humbled all over the place. Lately it's pro forma—possibly even mandatory— for politicians, athletes, celebrities and other public figures to be vocally and vigorously humbled by every honor awarded, prize won, job offered, record broken, pound lost, shout-out received, "like" copped and thumb upped. . . . We look up in beatific wonder at all we have accomplished. We bow our heads in recognition of this thing that's bigger than us, than our massive egos, and we're humbled by its immensity. And why not? It's got to be huge to eclipse *us*.

Echoing Chocano are the comments of Matthieu Richard in his acclaimed work, *Happiness.* In it, he not only parallels her comments but also points out the negative *social* implications when *humility*, as many formerly understood the term positively, is not embraced.

Our obsession with the image we have to project of ourselves is so strong that we have stopped questioning the validity of appearances and endlessly seek better ways to appear.

What images should we project? Politicians and movie stars have "media advisers" whose job it is to create a favorable image for their client with the general public, sometimes even teaching them how to smile. Newspapers are devoting more and more space to their "people pages," with grabby headlines on "people in the news," their ratings of who's "in" and who's "out." In all of this, what place is there for humility, a value so rare that it might almost be consigned to the museum of obsolete virtues? . . .

At the collective level, pride is expressed in the conviction of being superior to others as a nation or a race, of being the guardian of the true values of civilization, and of the need to impose this dominant "model" on "ignorant" peoples by any means available. This attitude often serves as a pretext for "developing" the resources of underdeveloped countries. The conquistadors and their bishops burned the vast Mayan and Aztec libraries of Mexico, of which barely a dozen volumes survive. . . . It was pride, above all, that allowed the Chinese to ignore the hundreds of thousands of volumes of philosophy housed in Tibetan monasteries before they demolished six thousand of centers of learning.

Humility as a value has a long history that needs to be revisited and valued anew for what it truly can mean in the way you live your life. A simple reflection on the concern with humility held by fourth-century Northern African and Persian Desert Fathers (*Abbas*) and Mothers (*Ammas*) bears this out. With respect to this group, poet Kathleen Norris, in her book *Acedia and Me*, notes, "[These early desert monks] valued humility as a tool for maintaining hope. While today the word *humility* may connote a placid servility in the face of mistreatment, its Latin origins suggest strength and fertility. The word comes from *hummus*, as in 'earth.' A humble person is one who accepts the paradox of being both 'great and small' and does not discount that hope which [philosopher] Kierkegaard terms 'possibility.'" Former host of the popular BBC radio program *The Living World*, Peter France, in his book *Patmos*, adds to this view by indicating that for this group of early monks, humility "was simply the rejection of self-centeredness. It was, and is, a powerful means of getting right with the world."

One of the ways such early monks sought to achieve this (and we—whether religious or not—can also learn from their example) is by setting aside periods of "alonetime." I define this term as those periods we spend in silence, and possibly solitude, to be mindful or meditate as well as when we are simply quietly reflective even when in a group. During such times, the goal is to be nonjudgmentally present to ourselves. Because of this we see our foibles as well as our gifts with a sense of clarity and equanimity. When this happens we open the door to humility because honesty gets an opportunity to come to the fore because of the space we provide in our consciousness. In providing this opening during quiet moments, we create a mental vacuum. Given this inner space, the "preconscious" or those cognitions (ways of thinking, perceiving, and understanding) lying just beyond our awareness are given room to rise to the fore for our examination. We are then faced with elements of life and our attitude toward ourselves and others that we may have set aside intentionally or unconsciously because, among other things, they can diminish or "prune" our prideful tendencies.

Information such as this engenders humility. Such an attitude then becomes transformative because when you take knowledge and you add humility, you get wisdom, and when you then add this wisdom to compassion, you get love. The new space within us that humility creates helps us unlearn what is no longer helpful. It also ideally positions us to welcome others into our interpersonal sphere without as many of our own needs or expectations. (This is the reason we will spend more time on the theme of "alonetime" later in this book.)

As also previously noted, a sense of ordinariness based on humility is sometimes associated with well-known spiritual figures, especially the present Dalai Lama and South Africa's Archbishop Desmond Tutu. Both are experienced as "ordinary" by those who meet them despite their status in the eyes of others. In the case of the Dalai Lama, people tell stories about his humility and ordinariness in many different instances. For example, in a book about him, *The Open Road*, author Pico Iyer writes, "'He did not claim to be, one never thought he was, perfect, or infallible,' my father had written at the time, 'but in his company I felt the freshness of immense personal purity'. . . and able to 'assume a variety of poses, utterly without affectation.'"

Both the Dalai Lama and Archbishop Tutu are constantly interested in the themes of "unlearning" and learning anew (topics that will also be discussed later in this chapter since they are important for the dynamic of ordinariness). In the words of the Dalai Lama, in *The Book of Joy*, "There is a Tibetan saying that wisdom is like rainwater—both gather in the low places. There is another saying that when the spring bloom comes, where does it start? Does it start in the hilltops or down in the valleys first? Growth begins first in the low places. So similarly if you remain humble, then there is the possibility to keep learning. So I often tell them that although I'm eighty years old, I still consider myself a student."

Their humility also comes through especially in their ability to laugh at themselves. One example of this is a vignette shared by Archbishop Desmond Tutu, also cited in *The Book of Joy*. He was on a flight home from Durban to Johannesburg during the anti-apartheid struggle. One of the flight attendants leaned over and asked him if he would autograph his book for one of the other passengers on board. In response, he admitted, "I tried to look humble and modest, although I was thinking in my heart that there were some people who recognized a good thing when they saw it." Then, as the attendant handed him the book to be signed and he was taking out his pen to do it, she said, "You are Bishop Muzorewa, aren't you?"

All of us, if we are honest, have had ourselves unveiled in such ways. One occurrence for me like this I have shared in previous works and lectures. The event simultaneously woke me up and brought a broad smile to my face. It was also an opportunity for me to grasp anew my respect for, but continued lack of, ability to incorporate humility in myself.

My daughter, son-in-law, and two grandchildren were sitting around the kitchen table for dinner. Once the meal was done, my daughter looked at her children and asked, "What are you particularly good at doing? In other words, what gifts do you think God has given to you so you can help others?"

My granddaughters love these types questions and launched into sharing a pretty full list of what modern positive psychology would call "signature strengths." After hearing this recitation by both of them, my son-in-law asked, "Well, what about humility? Neither of you mentioned that." To which my youngest granddaughter Emily immediately asked, "What's humility?"

My son-in-law is not so young that the Internet is his only source of information, so he said in reply, "Well, get the dictionary and let's look it up."

In response, the youngest scurried to find the dictionary, grabbed hold of it, and handed it to her dad. He found the entry for *humility*, read the definition out loud, and then asked, "Well, what person comes to mind when you hear this description?" To which all three of them immediately responded with great enthusiasm, "Mom-Mom!" referring to my wife. My son-in-law then asked, "Well, what about Pop-Pop?" They all shook their heads from side to side and said, "*Noooo*. Not Pop-Pop!"[1]

And so, I recognized when I heard this that the virtue of humility, while very valuable, is elusive even if you desire it— especially for "Pop-Pop!"

David Brooks, in his book on character formation, previously cited, echoes this with respect to his own life:

I was born with a natural disposition toward shallowness. I now work as a pundit and columnist. I'm paid to be a narcissistic blowhard, to volley my opinions, to appear more confident about them than I really am, to appear smarter than I really am, to appear better and more authoritative than I really am. I have to work harder than most people to avoid a life of smug superficiality. I've also become more aware that, like many people these days, I have lived a life of vague moral aspiration—vaguely wanting to be good, vaguely wanting to serve some larger purpose, while lacking a concrete moral vocabulary, a clear understanding of how to live a rich inner life, or even a clear knowledge of how character is developed and depth is achieved.

Shunryu Suzuki, a Sōtō Zen monk and spiritual guide who helped popularize Zen Buddhism in the United States and is renowned for founding one of the first Buddhist monasteries outside Asia, experienced for himself the great desire for humility but also wisely eventually questioned, as all of us must in our own case, the other less pure motives involved when seeking it. This challenge is related in the following story by David Chadwick in his quite balanced and rich biography of Suzuki, intriguingly entitled *The Crooked Cucumber*:

In his college dorm Shunryu awoke before the sun was up, quietly slipped on some loose work clothes, and tiptoed out of the sleeping quarters in the dark. He entered the latrine, which was lined on one side with squat toilets and a long urinal. . . . He crossed the room to a cabinet, took out bucket and rags, and there under the dim light of a kerosene lamp he began to clean. The room was always a stinking mess, not like those in the temples he'd lived in. Public toilets in Japan at that time were notorious for being undertended.

As a freshman at Komazawa University, Shunryu had taken it upon himself to do this onerous task before his classmates arose. As head monk at Keno-in, one of his responsibilities had been to clean the toilets and sinks, and he was determined that in the midst of his studies and activities in Tokyo he would not forget that he was a monk. "I wanted to practice true practice." . . .

It was especially important to him not to be seen. He was convinced that if others knew what he was up to, he would no longer be involved in pure practice. He'd listen for sounds of stirring and stick his head out in the hall periodically to see if a light was on. He particularly didn't want to be found out by Nukariya-sensei, the president of the school and his most important role model during this period. . . . He had impeccable humility and dignity. Visitors would often think he was a janitor. His presence further inspired Shunryu to take on this lowly duty. But if [Nukariya-sensei's] light was on, Shunryu would get flustered and make an escape.

At first he felt good about what he was doing, but more and more he analyzed the purity of his intention. He obsessed: Why am I doing this? Do I really like doing it without being noticed? Do I actually wish to be found out?

Suzuki's understanding deepened over his lifetime. It was evidenced especially in his interactions with his Zen students. He wanted them to be committed to Zazen (sitting meditation) and to living life fully without being deluded by anything or anyone—including, maybe *especially*, themselves. When they became proud or self-important he would poke a hole in their sense of pride or accomplishment, often with an off-handed remark. An example of this is the following interaction related by David Chadwick in the collection of stories about Suzuki shared in the little companion volume to his biography, *To Shine One Corner of the World*:

> Once while driving Suzuki Roshi back to San Francisco from Los Altos, I asked him if there was much hope for that handful of middle-aged, suburban housewives to accomplish anything as Zen students [such as we were]. After all, they only sat together once a week, unlike we students, who sat daily at Zen Center.
>
> He told me their understanding was "actually pretty good," and he noted, "They don't seem to suffer from arrogance."

Chadwick, in this collection of reflections and quotes, also shared another story that gives us insight into Suzuki:

> On a visit to the East Coast, Suzuki Roshi arrived at the meeting place of the Cambridge Buddhist Society to find everyone scrubbing down the interior in anticipation of his visit. They were surprised to see him, because he had written that he would arrive on the following day. He tied back the sleeves of his robe and insisted on joining the preparations "for the grand day of my arrival."

Suzuki also realized it was hard to have a major impact on our own habits but he advocated working on them because the failures experienced would reduce egoism. It would also help build character in the process. Seeking humility doesn't result in success—it often ends in our seeing, instead, our lack of it when we fail.

Another major challenge with valuing humility, one of the main underpinnings of ordinariness, is that, especially today, most of us have been taught:

- "Image" is more important than reality.
- Humility is really a version of poor self-esteem, inadequate self-confidence, a lack of personal worth, or being unduly vulnerable.
- Showing what you know is more important than the vulnerability necessary for new wisdom through admitting ignorance and opening the door to "unlearning."
- Self-absorption is natural (and should be enhanced online in how we electronically communicate much of our daily activities in ways that they deserve to be in everyone's ship's log).

In the book, *The Cure of the Self: Self-Awareness, Egotism, and the Quality of Human Life*, by well-respected psychology scholar Mark Leary, the author points out that the self is not something evil. Instead, he indicates that seeking a greater sense of awareness through self-reflection also has its downsides. However, by knowing this, we can limit or avoid them. In his words:

. . . the same ability to self-reflect that makes us wonderfully human and underlies the best features of civilization also creates havoc by fostering selfishness, suffering, troubled relationships, disastrous decisions, and behavior that is dangerous to ourselves and to other people. The self is at once our greatest ally and our fiercest enemy, and many of the biggest struggles that people face in life are directly or indirectly the doing of the self.

In facing the difficulties inherent in being self-reflective, Leary encourages "ego-skepticism" because his research and study have shown that "people overestimate how egocentric other people are while underestimating their own egocentrism." In addition, he feels it is important that in recognizing our uniqueness—what I would term "our ordinary selves"—we can then better appreciate that our perspective on the world is both unique and open to challenge when we represent it as the total truth for everyone. He recognizes that in most cases, indeed, we act not out of conscious malice but with an underlying sense that we are correct in our understanding and perception of people and events. In his work, he indicates that if we stop feeling we are infallible in such instances, then we can not only be more open to other views and new knowledge and unlearning but also not waste so much energy trying to defend our mental image of life.

In taking on such a philosophy, he emphasizes we must do it with a spirit of "self-compassion." By this he does not mean "self-pity, self-indulgence, or self-centeredness." Rather, to his mind, it involves "accepting the fact that one is not perfect and, thus, will invariably experience failures, setbacks, and losses." After all, he says, we need to have the gentle recognition that "we are, after all, only human." This approach will help us to be less "egoic" in life, prevent us from being as biased, and open us to a spirit of unlearning that appreciates that our views are the result of experiences within a certain range, and open us to new learning by *unlearning*.

ENHANCING A SPIRIT
OF UNLEARNING

In her fascinating biography, *Henry David Thoreau: A Life*, Laura Dassow Walls writes:

> Thoreau struggled all his life to find a voice that could be heard despite the din of cynicism and the babble of convention. . . . Thoreau earned the devotion of friends who saw in him no saint, but something perhaps more rare: a humane being living a whole human life. . . . I began this biography to return to the figure who opened up that space for independent thinking, to learn how he had opened up that space for himself. . . . it was clear to him that the American Revolution was incomplete: inequality was rife, materialism was rampant, and the American economy was wholly dependent upon slavery. Yet in a terrible irony, his elders seemed content to let this state of things, from which they all benefited, continue. No, they were not to be trusted; he must try the experiment for himself.

What Thoreau recognized is that while some others felt they were operating with a sense of enlightenment rather than entitlement, it wasn't true—even if, *especially* if, it was accepted as the common wisdom of the day. Instead, he not only wanted to question their "wisdom" but also, in the process, his own up to that point.

People are often concerned about the negative impact of their ignorance. They feel it is what they *don't* know that will hurt them and this is, of course, true to a certain extent. However, I believe that an even more insidious danger than ignorance is when, through a lack of humility, we think we already know something that we actually don't fully understand. The real wisdom that marks ordinariness appreciates this reality.

At times we can be so stubborn or "hard-hearted" that even when presented with contrary information, we "dig in our heels" and hold onto our opinions rather than being open enough to let in new information that may prove us wrong. The following delightful story by Indian psychologist and spiritual writer Anthony de Mello illustrates this well. A woman suddenly stops a man walking down the street and says:

> "Henry, I am so happy to see you after all these years! My, how you have changed."
>
> "I remember you as being tall and you seem so much shorter now."
>
> "Good grief how you have changed in five years!"

Finally, the man got a chance to interject: "But my name isn't Henry!"

To which the persistent woman calmly responded: "Oh, so you changed your name, too!"[2]

What is being humorously described in this story is what psychologists refer to as "confirmation bias." It is something all of us more or less do at times, so it is quite natural and common, which makes it so dangerous to unlearning and openness. In his book, *The Science of Fear*, Daniel Gardner expands on this when he notes,

> Once a belief is in place, we screen what we see and hear in a biased way that ensures our beliefs are "proven" correct. Psychologists have also discovered that people are vulnerable to something called group polarization—which means that when people who share beliefs get together in groups, they become more convinced that their beliefs are right and they become more extreme in their views. Put confirmation bias, group polarization, and culture together, and we start to understand why people can come to completely different views about which risks are frightening and which aren't worth a second thought.

All through the history of the human race we have heard stories of people being asked to let go, unlearn, reform, renew, and be open to recognize and embrace an identity that is more in line with who they could become rather than who they have settled for being because of the presence of pressures of society or family, anxiety or ignorance. For instance, in the Hebrew Scriptures we see how Abram is called to let go of the identity he had in order to become open to the person he could and should be (Abraham). Likewise, his wife Sarai is asked to let go of her limited sense of self to become Sarah, a woman filled with new potential.

Like them and others throughout history who were not lured away from self-exploration and development, we are now called to unlearn much of what we have absorbed that is untrue about ourselves so we can embrace our "ordinary selves." This will allow us to be open to new realities and new possibilities, and to become more deeply aware of our own true "name" and identity. We can then model this for others so they can also be empowered to see and take their places of dignity in the world. Yet, as we have emphasized, this is contrary to what many leaders in society might claim: It doesn't take arrogance to claim or reclaim ourselves, it takes the elusive and rare virtue of humility that is so mistaken and misunderstood today.

Today, it is no wonder, then, that the humility that is necessary to see ourselves in a clear and honest way is so difficult to comprehend since it is very different from the way it is portrayed. Moreover, its presence in us, as we saw in Nukariya-sensei's effect on Shunryu Suzuki's commitment to clean the toilets while everyone was sleeping, can have a very important positive impact on others as well.

In the words of Douglas Abrams, who served as editor and compiler of the book on the Dalai Lama and Archbishop Desmond Tutu previously cited (*The Book of Joy*):

> Humility as an attitude is also essentially focused on others and their well-being. Studies in social psychology have found that people who overvalue themselves present a higher than average tendency toward aggression. These studies also highlight the relationship between humility and the faculty of forgiveness. People who consider themselves superior judge the faults of others more harshly and consider them to be less favorable.
>
> Paradoxically, humility promotes strength of character; the humble person makes decisions on the basis of what he believes to be right and sticks by them without concern for his own image or the opinions of others. . . . This resolve has nothing to do with obstinacy and stubbornness. It arises from the clear perception of a meaningful goal. It is pointless trying to persuade the woodsman with a perfect knowledge of the forest to take the path leading to a cliff.

This is the reason why humility really involves not hiding our talents and burying our gifts. Augustine of Hippo knew this and in his fifth-century work, *City of God*, wrote: "Do you wish to be great? Then begin by being. Do you desire to create a vast and lofty fabric? Think first about the foundations of humility. The higher your structure is to be, the deeper must be its foundation." This ancient call to humility opens us up to see that we are surrounded by "teachers" if we have the right perspective.

Once, when teaching a graduate course on the integration of psychology and classic spirituality, I noticed a fascinating dynamic between two of the students. One was a Buddhist and the other an Evangelical Christian. The Buddhist modeled a sense of serenity and the Evangelical Christian was passionate and would sometimes be quite expressive. I noticed when she would be so outgoing with her feelings and opinions, it would be quite disturbing for the Buddhist who was sitting right in front of me. In response, he would make facial expressions that only I could see. I kept my observations of his reactions to myself.

Then, one day, the student who was so effusive became so excited about something that she actually wound up throwing something at the board just missing me. She, of course, was mortified and later shared with me that she recognized her need to look at her behavior, which I reinforced because I knew with some mentoring her deep passion could find greater focus and produce better results for her and those with whom she interacted.

However, after this outburst on her part, the young Buddhist counseling student in front of me could not contain his disdain for her behavior. And so, I felt it was time to "take advantage" of his reaction this time to help him search further within himself, and asked him at the end of class if he would remain.

When all had left, I said to him, "You noticed the behavior of the student who threw something at the board." He responded quite vehemently that he did and the psychological dike broke open as he laid out his negative feelings toward her. Once he was done, in a low voice I said to him, "She is your spiritual guide." In response you could see the incredulous look on his face before he commented, "I'll have to think about that." To which I said, "I didn't ask you to think about it. She is your spiritual director." And at that I walked out, leaving him to reflect on what I had said so firmly.

My point to this very psychologically and spiritually mature student was that he was ready to see that anything and anyone who was able to elicit that much negative emotion was actually a "teacher" to him about what he found most upsetting, fearful, anxiety-provoking, or a cause for anger rather than sorrow. When we can listen to those we find we don't like in a way that calls us deeper to examine our own virtues, much can be learned about ourselves and little is left for projection of blame onto others. Moreover, as the Dalai Lama once noted, "A person who practices compassion and forgiveness has greater inner strength, whereas aggression is usually a sign of weakness." If this lesson could be learned by us and today's politicians it would be a more peaceful world guided forth by more humble leaders.

As I have now passed the age of seventy, I had to smile when I read the following words of Polish-born rabbi, theologian, and philosopher, Abraham Joshua Heschel: "When I was young, I used to admire intelligent people; as I grow older, I admire kind people."

As we have seen, humility also helps us avoid being involved in the errors of over-self-confidence or extreme self-doubt. It is tied to helping us see more clearly, to embrace the truth—both positive and negative—about ourselves, to try to be our *ordinary* self with others, and—when confronted by a world of exaggeration, unnecessary complexity, and narcissism—to embrace another rare virtue: *simplicity*.

TWO

Travel Lightly: Simplicity and Letting Go

You don't need to be a sorcerer to cast
a spell over yourself by saying, "This is
who I am. I can do nothing about it."
—French philosopher Alain (Émile-August
Chartres)

Do I contradict myself?
Very well, then I contradict myself.
(I am large, I contain multitudes.)
—Walt Whitman, *Song of Myself*

In her little booklet, *Reflections on Simplicity*, Elaine Prevallet notes the following section from an old Shaker hymn purported to be written by Elder Brackett in 1848 in Alfred, Maine:

'Tis the gift to be simple;

'Tis the gift to be free;

'Tis the gift to come down where we ought to be . . ."

She then follows this quote by offering a consideration of simplicity that could well be said of both "ordinariness" and "humility," aptly noting,

> It is good to begin by remembering that simplicity is a gift, for a gift cannot be grasped. And simplicity, in its own way, eludes our grasp. It seems, under scrutiny, to transmute itself into other virtues, now appearing as poverty of spirit, humility, dependence, abandonment, and then appearing as single-mindedness, integrity, purity of heart. One sees it more clearly when not looking directly at it.

If ordinariness is a forgotten virtue and humility an elusive one, simplicity is certainly one that is wistfully viewed as surprisingly unattainable or impractical in modern life. Today, many of us tend to seesaw between envying those who live a simple life on the one hand and feeling it would be quite easy "if only" our life didn't have so many responsibilities on the other.

Despite this sense of simplicity as an unattainable dream, there are persons with very full, demanding and complex lives who see simplicity as an underlying attitude to behold and embrace, no matter how many challenges face them. Once again, Pico Iyer notes this with respect to the current Dalai Lama:

> He really does live simply, decorating his bedroom when he travels with just a few pictures of his teachers and his family and a portable radio. He really is a full-time, lifelong student of the Buddha, who taught him that nearly everything

is illusory and passing, not least that being who declares everything is illusory and passing. And he really does aspire, as every monk does, to a simplicity *that lies not before complexity but on the far side of it, have not dodged experience but subsumed it.* (Italics added.)

As is especially the case with respect to humility, being ordinary without embracing simplicity is almost impossible.

Clark Strand, in his book *The Wooden Bowl*, offers meditation as simply a place to relax, breathe deeply, and enjoy the simplicity of your life in ways that allow you to share it with others by opening up interpersonal space for them. He credits this sense, to a great degree, to his first teacher, Deh Chun. This mentor was an elderly Chinese hermit who lived his final years in Monteagle, Tennessee. Some of what Strand deeply felt about this simple sage is contained in the following reflection:

> When I consider the years of our association, the most remarkable thing is that I cannot recall any particular thing I learned from him. I can't point to a particular conversation we had and say, "Well, you know, then Deh Chun said such and such and everything was clear." At the time, *nothing* was clear. When I think back on it now, I realize that his entire teaching consisted of being in the present moment, with nothing else whatsoever added on.
>
> Being with Deh Chun was like dropping through a hole in everything that the world said was important—education, progress, money, sex, prestige. It was like discovering

that nothing else mattered and all I needed was *now*—the moment—to survive. Sitting there in the little house, listening to the water boil, to the twigs crackling in the wood stove, I was temporarily removed from the game. That was the genius of his teaching, that he could bring forth that transformation without even saying a word.

His was a state of complete simplicity. Like water, the direction of his life was downward, always seeking lower ground. . . .

Long after his death, it is finally clear to me that he taught only by example. Recently, a friend of mine said of a certain Catholic priest, "He practices what he preaches, so he doesn't have to preach so loud." Deh Chun practiced so well he didn't have to preach at all.

Simplicity, and one of its closest relatives, asceticism, call us to drop what is unnecessary or requiring too much energy. This is done not to avoid the necessary challenges or miss the joyful experiences of life but, to the contrary, to clean one's psychological and sensual palates. As Ricard notes in his book *Happiness,* "Simplifying one's life to extract its quintessence is the most rewarding of all the pursuits I have undertaken. It doesn't mean giving up what is truly beneficial, but finding out what really matters and what brings lasting fulfillment, joy, serenity, and, above all, the irreplaceable boon of altruistic love. It means transforming oneself to better transform the world."

Asceticism helps us increase our sensitivity to life's "small" gifts. It also has the benefit of helping us to appreciate ordinariness rather than inflate ourselves in ways that society feels is necessary if—according to some—we are to grasp what is best for, and due to, us. Sometimes, simplicity even trumps education because it engenders wisdom and another seemingly rare gift today: *common sense.*

The following, no doubt apocryphal, story I heard long ago, upon arriving in Baltimore for a teaching position at Loyola University Maryland. It has been a reminder to me when I get on my high horse because I fear being small, ordinary. I try to remember it when egoism seems to drive me to puff myself up rather than "simply" flow with who I am. Although this story was probably fabricated, it has stuck with me, and I have also tried to remember and apply its basic message whenever I have felt lost or too wrapped up in my own thinking. It is a dialogue between an old fellow who lived in Little Italy just outside Baltimore's Inner Harbor area and his son.

He owned a shop, and one of his three adult children, who was an accountant, would come in each week to help his father with the business. This was nice of him, but he also tended at times to be a bit self-important, like many of us, and arrogant. During one such episode, he said to his father, "Dad, how do you know what your profits are? You've got your cash in the cash register, your debits in a cigar box, and your accounts payable on a spindle. How do you know what your profits are?"

Finally, his father had experienced enough and instructed his son to sit down. Once he was seated, his father looked him directly in the eyes and said, "When I came to this country forty years ago from Italy I had only the pants I was wearing. Now your brother is a doctor, your sister a teacher, and you are an accountant. I have a house, a car, and a business and they're all paid for. So, you add them all up, subtract the pants, and there's your profit!"

When encountering such simplicity in life and in others we meet, as in the case of anything quietly dramatic, it can also be quite a jarring experience for us. Maybe that is why we avoid it or claim it is impossible to attain. If we are honest, it forces us to see our attitude toward "needs" we felt were essential but were only made so by conditioning. William Langewiesche, in his book *Sahara Unveiled*, describes this beautifully in the following way in his use of the desert as a metaphor for life:

> The Sahara is the earth stripped of its gentleness, a place that consumes the careless and the unlucky. But all you need to navigate it is a suitcase, a bit of cash, and occasional bus ticket, the intention to move on. Such simplicity appeals to me. . . . The Sahara has horizons so bare that drivers mistake stones for diesel trucks, and so lonely that migrating birds land beside people just for the company. The certainty of such sparseness can be a lesson. I lay in Algiers in a hotel in a storm, thinking there is no better sound than the splash of rain. The desert teaches by taking away.

Encountering simplicity embodied in another person can cause us, as I previously noted, to have a sense of wistfulness when we compare how we are leading our own lives today to how those who are truly ordinary and simple lead theirs. George Crane, a former correspondent for overseas news agencies, befriended and wrote a book with a Chan (Chinese Zen) master named Tsung Tsai. The two traveled together to China. The last stop on the way home was in Hong Kong. Tsung Tsai wanted to meet with a fellow monk he knew before fleeing China amidst the Cultural Revolution.

During the trip, Crane had ample time to more deeply reflect on his own life when he was in the presence of this Chan master and his fellow monk. Toward the end of the book, *Bones of the Master*, Crane shares a reflection on his own life that struck me personally. In it he compares himself with Tsung Tsai and Tsung's old friend in terms of the virtues of simplicity, ordinariness, and acceptance and, in return, receives a poignant response from the master:

> *Two old men*, I thought. *Simple as uncarved wood.* They had none of my guilt and anger; none of my arrogance or sarcasm. There was calmness about them, a startling sense of completion. They were, it seemed, without yearning, something unimaginable in men. They embodied Zen: *Be happy to live. Be happy to die. Do your work and pass on.* They were beyond my fear that the universe was without meaning, beyond my grasping

for understanding. . . . I thought about confessing, telling them all the awful things I had done. My deceits and cheats, as Tsung Tsai called them. *Cheat who?* Tsung Tsai would have asked. *Everybody, Tsung Tsai. Everybody.* When I looked up, they were staring at me with dark, wet eyes.

"Georgie, Georgie." Tsung Tsai sighed. "You so sad. Sometimes so foolish. So much worry. Your fox mind."

Today, we are shocked by simplicity and ordinariness. Just like "Georgie" we are enmeshed in the fabricated complexities of life rather than guided by the virtues of ordinariness, humility, and simplicity. Like Georgie, we have an overly complicated and overly self-involved and critical "fox mind." No matter how bright or experienced in studying human nature we are, the presence of people of simplicity upends our sense of things. When we do experience such virtues, it has us fall back on ourselves with the recognition of how we have become so jaded with the philosophies, positioning, falsehood, and overly self-protective aggression that surrounds and is within us.

A psychologist who studied people of rural India admitted as much to author Andrew Harvey, in the following passage from what many consider to be a modern spiritual classic, *Journey in Ladakh*:

My research takes me every day to a new village to interview someone, to talk with a family. And I have seen people of nearly every kind now. I have been to the most remote villages,

I have talked with lamas and Westernized Ladakhis and old women and young shepherds. I ask all sorts of questions. It is strange for a cynical psychologist to spend every day with people that seem, as far as I can judge, to have little interest in deceiving or impressing you. . . . And it is strange for me too to be among people who for the most part are happy. Don't get me wrong—this is a harsh land. It is hard to get the crops to grow here on rocky mountainsides, it is hard to survive the solitudes of the winter and the lonely places. . . . But most of these people live simply and unsentimentally, they live with few prides, few vanities. They are tolerant to their old people, to their children, to each other. . . . I have seen very little cruelty. Once I saw a child tormenting a dog. That's about all—in three years . . . when you see and feel this peace, this dignity, day after day in the most ordinary situations, in the way in which an old woman will make you tea, in the way she smiles at you from the fields, in the frankness of her answers to your questions. . . . I do not understand it but I am moved by it.

Such a moving experience as that shared by this psychologist, and recorded for us by Harvey, is one that ordinariness, fostered by both humility and simplicity, can produce in those who encounter us when we are in our unvarnished, non-defensive ordinary self as well. Still, for this to occur, we must be willing to psychologically—and some would say spiritually—"travel lightly."

Elaine Prevallet, in her Pendle Hill pamphlet *Reflections on Simplicity*, once again makes the following connection nicely in her discussion of the desire to become more aware of our need to possess material things but also, even more than that, our psychological needs, so we can live out of a spirit of ordinariness, humility, and simplicity. In line with this she notes:

[W]e also learn, as life educates us, that far more difficult than material possession is personal affective possessiveness: to love unpossessingly, to let go a love, to regard enough whatever anyone is willing to give me of their love, to receive it gratefully as the gift it is and not to demand more. That is a far more difficult kind of letting go. One grows aware that the root system of the weed of possessiveness is deep and devious, that it grows unnoticed beneath the surface, winding around the inner reaches of the heart, tangling, meshing, binding. Other sources of security are revealed to us: a talent, a job, a position we've held and come to identify with, to know we're good at.

Gradually that comes to take possession of us, to dominate and control us, to provide us, very subtly, with a source of security. Then the prospect of losing it becomes very frightening and we hang on yet more tightly. We have placed our security in something without even knowing it, and certainly without clearly willing it. And on, through the successive detachments life asks of us, each exposing in a new way something we clung to without knowing it because we took it

for granted: health, being able to do this or that, being *able*—
even to walk, or to see, or to hear, or to speak. They were all
gifts and we didn't know it. We thought we were the masters;
we thought we owned them. So who is the master we serve?

We may start to get rid of material possessions, find we
can live with very little, and so begin to fancy ourselves de-
tached. . . . We must do the outer actions: we must strip down,
give away, let go, do what we can. We must make the outside of the cup clean. But we mustn't make the mistake of
stopping there . . . assuming the inner reality . . . necessarily
follows because we did the other thing right.

During times of war, greed, and confusion, the search for simplicity and a recapturing of the ordinary self often intensifies.
After World War II, people sought out monasteries to live out
a life that they perceived would remove distractions and provide a setting where they could find meaning. As a part of this
search they also wished to find themselves again. If they were
really only running away, they eventually left the monastery or
became disillusioned anew when their honeymoon with silence
and solitude wore off.

Today, a similar pattern seems to be evidencing itself in certain corners of China with respect to Buddhism. As prosperity
rises in China, some are reporting that it feels "hollow" to them
in some way. This is compounded when shopkeepers realize
they must bribe government officials in various ways if they
are to continue to operate and financially flourish. To some this

goes against the ancient teachings of right living and morality. In an article on this response,[1] Ian Johnson reports from Yixing, China about a woman named Shin Ying who was a successful shop owner who became disillusioned by the move to modernism that was so alien to the teachings of her parents.

"You just feel disappointed at some of the dishonest conduct in society," she said.

Then, five years ago, a Buddhist organization from Taiwan . . . began building a temple on the outskirts of her city. . . . She began attending its meetings and studying its texts—and it changed her life.

She and her husband, a successful businessman, started living more simply. They gave up luxury goods and made donations to support poor children. And before the temple opened last year, she left her convenience store to manage a tea shop near the temple, pledging the proceeds to charity.

Across China, millions of people like Ms. Shen have begun to participate in faith-based organizations like Fo Guang Shan. They aim to fill what they see as a moral vacuum left by attacks on traditional values over the past century.

And so, in a world that would have us make money at any cost, carry titles to impress, as well as seek successes and roles as the price of entry into acceptance and a temporary feeling of security, true simplicity would be helpful. Yet, if we are to embrace ordinariness along with humility and simplicity in life, we need to learn to "travel lightly." This means unlearning what prevents us from living this way. In the case of Shin Ying, even when she opened the tea house, she was tempted to use inferior oil as a way of making more money for the temple. Yet, as Ian Johnson reports, "her husband objected. China is rife with scandals about restaurants using unsafe or cheap ingredients, and he argued that good Buddhists should set a better example."

David S. Brown, author of *Paradise Lost: A Life of F. Scott Fitzgerald*, pointed out that Fitzgerald, the author of the novels *The Great Gatsby* and *Tender Is the Night*, held a similar feeling about Americans during his own time:

> In a sense, we have always understood Fitzgerald to be a student of the past who took up as his special expertise the Jeffersonian "pursuit of happiness" hypothesis known today as the "American Dream." For today's readers, the "Dream" might signify a private, temporal triumph—a good job, a well-furnished home, and a comfortable retirement. To Fitzgerald, however, the promise of America meant something much different. Like the Founders, he saw America as a continent of possibilities, a place to escape the Old World's rigidly enforced class structures and adopt new identities. Put another way, his emphasis was not on the *accumulating* but rather on the *becoming*.

And so, traveling lightly means not only letting go of unnecessary possessions but also old inner habits that prevent us from being simply and ethically persons without guile who can purify the world for ourselves and for others as well. Although this takes a bit of doing, it is possible.

TRAVELLING LIGHTLY

Being Comfortable in Our Own "Psychological Clothes"

Coming home to our ordinary selves can be dramatic, the result of a surprising event, or a very slow process. Michael McGregor, in his splendid biography of minimalist poet Robert Lax, said of him, "After years of wearing other people's outfits, he had found his own comfortable clothes."

McGregor also wrote to me about his book and Lax in response to a reflection I sent to him about his work:

One of my main motivations for writing the book was a deep belief that a life like Lax's should be known to more people, not as a life to be emulated necessarily but as an inspiration to think differently and trust in values other than those we see promoted incessantly in our culture. Simplicity, creativity, faith, mindful attention to life in all of its particulars, pursuit of high meaning, eschewing of mainstream ideas of "success" and "gain"—these characteristics and values are more necessary now than ever, and Lax embodied all of them while being loving and joyful and humble. I'm pleased to know his way of being has touched you too.

Insight to accomplishing this may occur in different ways. For instance, philosopher Gabriel Maral reported, "I know by my own experience how, from a stranger met by chance, there may come an irresistible appeal which overturns the habitual perspectives, just as a gust of wind might tumble down the panels of a stage set."

No matter the cause, when we begin to discover who we are, whatever the impetus of doing so, we find other identities must be shed—even if we have grown accustomed to them or others like them. They may even have become habitual or attractive in some way to us along the way. But if we are to find both ourselves and a mission in life that flows out of it, as Parker Palmer emphasizes in his book *Let Your Life Speak*, "discard them we must."

The fear of being our own—ordinary—selves is not caused solely by outside influences and the prohibitions of family and society. As existential philosophers note, it can also come from within, and we must face this challenging reality. Karl Jaspers pointed out that what really scares us is the emptiness in front of us and our freedom to fill it. Sartre, on a slightly more positive note, indicated that a good life is *both* possible and painful at times. But in the end, according to both men, the choice is ours—*if we take it.*

I remember studying to be a priest. It had been an almost lifelong pursuit that was reinforced by my parents and many around me. To my mind, it was clearly the thing for me to do. But was it clearly me mindfully pursuing what I felt would be a way to flourish and to share my life? At one point, it became evident that it was not. However, there were a number of people who were close to me, in my family and group of friends, who were just as adamant that I should stay the course.

When I finally made the move to leave these studies, it occurred to me that because I had been on this journey in my mind for so long, what would I do now? There was no specific vocation other than priesthood before me. In my first job interview after leaving potential priesthood, I began to recognize that while I had made a step out of priesthood, the idea of flourishing in the service of others was still a burning and freely embraced desire. However, I was so wary of once again going with the flow of others' desires that I thought I was being courageous in taking a step in a totally seemingly opposite direction: business. This time, under the influence of my oldest brother, I applied for a position at Continental Can Company as a "leadership trainee." The interview's close showed me once again that the road I could vaguely see ahead of me was not to be one in the field of business.

Right after the interview was over a friend asked, "Well, how did it go?" I said, "Well, it was humming along pretty well until I was asked, "In essence, why do you want to be a sales executive for this company?" "And what did you say?" "I said, 'because my family has long been committed to public service.'" I thought my friend would burst his side laughing as he said, "Well, I can't imagine why that wouldn't sink the basket on a job where you are being paid to sell a product to customers whether or not they needed or wanted it."

Reading Parker Palmer's book, *Let Your Life Speak*, years later, I had to laugh when he wrote, "[there are] moments when it is clear—if I have the eyes to see—that the life I am living is not the same as the life that wants to live in me. In those moments I sometimes catch a glimpse of my true life, a life hidden like the river beneath the ice. . . . I wonder [at such times]: What am I meant to do? Who am I meant to be?"

In psychotherapy, I have found that patients will often take one or the other side of the extreme when faced with the dilemma of such questions. They feel either they need what amounts to magic or a miracle to change or they are doomed to follow the unhelpful road that brought them to treatment in the first place. Part of psychotherapy's overarching goal is to help them walk a road that may be difficult but will, in the process, lead to a more satisfactory life. Central to this journey is a letting go and leaving behind what is unnecessary in order to "travel light."

Alan Jones relates this message in the following way in his book, *Soul Making*:

It is said that during an uprising in India late in the last century when British service families had to be evacuated, the road was strewn with such things as stuffed owls and Victorian bric-a-brac. I have no idea what the late twentieth century equivalent of a stuffed owl is, but no doubt our path will be just as littered with such "necessities." We will have to learn to travel light.

I would add to this that in the spirit of ordinariness, traveling light requires *kenosis* and unlearning as a way to open ourselves up for new possibility.

Kenosis is the Greek word for the process of emptying yourself. When poet Robert Lax, was interviewed by S.T. Georgiou for his book, *The Way of the Dreamcatcher*, he asked about *kenosis*. Lax said,

> Figuratively speaking, kenosis has to do with the idea that when you give, you let go, you empty yourself, and as you do so, you place yourself in the position to receive more. It's cyclic, much like our breathing—you exhale, or give out, then you inhale, and take in. Giving-receiving, receiving-giving. I can't receive anything from nature if I've evaporated the sea with a burst of white-hot words. But with one cool little drop of a word there's plenty of room to reflect. The whole thing to do is to refrain from blocking the flow. In the kenotic mode, any trace of ego disappears right into what you are doing. You don't struggle with it anymore because you become an open door, a channel, a conduit. Like I've said, an unobstructed garden hose is a clear channel—it just does its work.

When prompted further by Georgiou with respect to the development of Lax's early decision to try to live and write with a sense of simplicity, Lax responded, "I have tried to live focusing on what is essential. When life is uncluttered, when verse is uncluttered, there is a great freedom of movement and clearer vision. As they say, when the water is still, you can see right down to the bottom. We all pay homage to clarity."

Yet, to my mind, for such clarity to exist—especially about our ordinary self—there is much that has accumulated in our self-image that needs to be released. The question that remains is: Will we see such accumulations for what they are? Will we be willing to ask ourselves:

> *What chains us in different, possibly familiar and comfortable ways, to an image that prevents our ordinary selves from being freed. In other words, will we choose to remain oblivious to our current dominance by invisible mental and social puppeteers or step out into the new, unknown, and possibly unbelievable?*

Elias Canetti, in *Notes from Hampstead*, writes, "I should like to contain everything within myself yet stay quite simple. That is hard. For I don't want to lose this variety, much as I wish to be simple." In his article "Simplicity and Ordinariness: The Climate of Early Cistercian Hagiography," Chrysogonus Waddell seems to recognize this process in how the contemplative Thomas Merton sought simplicity amidst the delicate differences and complexities of the incoming knowledge of so many disparate sources. He wrote about Merton, "He had a special gift for quickly assimilating large amounts of material, sorting out the essential from the trappings, and developing it further with the help of his own insights." In my own reflection on the development of Merton's writings and journals, I believe he became better and better at this, primarily, I think because Merton began to be less fooled by the narrowness of some of his views. In addition, he recognized that in being open to the fresh air of new wisdom it becomes possible to absorb and be comfortable with finding out that the reputation you have with yourself is, at the very least, always incomplete.

Uncovering Subtle Styles of Defense

"What's it like to be free?" I asked a friend who had been locked up for thirty-four months for a white collar crime. He responded in the following simple, concrete, understated, yet powerful way: "In the mornings I can have a hot cup of coffee when I want it. I can walk over and open up closed doors without having to ask someone for permission to do it." Would that we had that sense of gratefulness for the little things of life and appreciated the doors of life that are open to us, as well as the ones that we have *psychologically* closed up.

The virtues of humility and simplicity and a spirit of unlearning are good gateways to discovering and embracing our ordinary selves rather than remaining unknowing slaves to habit, culture, and limited or distorted self-definition. These virtues can open "doors" to self-knowledge and self-recognition in ways that have long been the cornerstones of personal freedom.

Embracing ordinariness, so we can flow in life rather than drift or be pulled in other directions, is one of the steps we need to take to be more sensitive to our subtle styles of defensiveness. This tendency to block out some information and give more import to other data is often referred to as being "characterological" in nature and may be best understood by viewing what psychologists have uncovered from working with persons who have personality styles that are inappropriate yet quite ingrained. Persons in these categories are very difficult to treat because they believe that there is nothing wrong with them. In their minds, it is the world that needs to change! This is most easily observed in individuals suffering from a personality disorder who are well-known personalities in politics, entertainment, and business.

Such persons have ingrained, lifelong personality styles of dealing with their lives and the world which they don't find uncomfortable in themselves but which cause others problems (which in turn may make life tough for them when people react in a negative fashion). This is very unlike persons suffering from the disorder we used to refer to as "neurotic." Persons in this category are well aware of their problems and are distressed over them.

Consequently, real care needs to be taken with persons in the characterological category. The therapist, mentor, or spiritual guide must not assume that the behavior presented is causing the person inner turmoil and that is why he or she wishes to change it. In addition, one must carefully work to show the person that he or she will have to pay the price if this type of destructive behavior continues—even though it might not presently be seen in this light.

To illustrate, a young woman in her twenties came in for treatment at the urging of her father. Once we were done with the opening greeting and I had some basic identifying data, I asked her to explain what she wanted from our time together.

In response, she launched into a story of how she had begun college this past fall. She said that as a freshman she tended to socialize with sophomores, went to parties all the time, drank a great deal of alcohol, let her studies slide, and almost failed out of school. Then, in the beginning of sophomore year she said she did get expelled for breaking a number of rules, rarely showing up for class, and having all "F" grades in her courses. Because of this, her parents lost thousands of dollars in tuition.

When she returned home, she continued her extreme "social" life, again with bouts of heavy drinking and wild hours. Late one night, after her parents were in bed, she even brought the young man she was with that evening home to spend the night in her room with her. She said they planned to wake up early so as not to get caught, but since they both had so much to drink, they overslept. In the morning, her mother came down and upon finding her in bed with this man, became furious, chasing her around the house.

Having told me this story, she sat back waiting for my response. During the telling of the story, when I looked at her face, I didn't see any sense of remorse, being upset, or recognition of her having made a mistake. Instead, there was a general relaxed demeanor interspersed with smiles and light laughter.

Given this, I looked at her and gently said, "It sounds like you feel you have been having quite a good time." She seemed startled, perhaps because of the previous disapproving responses she had received from her family, and said, "Excuse me?"

I said, "It seems like you have been having a lot of fun, a generally wonderful time. Is that not so?"

She finally collected herself and said, "Well, 'er, yes, I guess so."

I then replied, "Well, we don't treat that here."

After another pause, she replied with a somewhat distraught look on her face, "But don't you realize that because of all of this, the ceiling is falling in on my head at home?"

"Ah," I responded, "Now, that kind of problem we *do* treat." What I was trying to do was not get caught in the trap of responding to her as others had mistakenly done. One of the roles of a therapist, coach, or mentor is to be a different person to the patient or person seeking guidance. By doing this, one is more likely to break through the normal crust of denial and avoidance, name the behavior for the destructive or distorted nature it is, and then look at more productive alternatives.

This illustration is especially relevant here, because it shines a light on the fact that a style of interaction that is beyond our level of awareness can be very destructive or limiting. In addition, it is important for us to recognize that all of us have unproductive characterological styles which, while perhaps not as extreme as the case just presented, can be just as hidden and quietly destructive to our recognizing our own narrative in ways that make it difficult to not only find our way in life but also share it with others in a way that enables them to find and embrace their generative own ordinary selves.

Even the most sensitive and self-aware individuals can miss so much. I remember a talented psychologist approaching me once in the hallway at the university where I was teaching at the time and asking if we could chat for a moment. After we went into my office, I closed the door, motioned for him to sit down, sat down across from him, and simply said, "What's up?"

He then related to me how he was having problems with colleagues, friends, and even his own children, who would roll their eyes when he started sharing his woes with them. Because of this, he said that he had decided to re-enter therapy; he hadn't been in therapy since he was in training to be a psychotherapist himself.

After he finished, I told him that as a friend I was glad he was going to treat himself to some time to reflect and have the support of being in a therapeutic relationship on the receiving end. I also commended him for his courage in doing this.

"Courage?" he responded. "Yes, I feel that, as you know, when we enter therapy it provides a safe place that we can feel free to be ourselves and know that it will be all right. However, again, as you are aware, no matter how much the environment is toxic, the therapist can best help us with what it is that *we* are doing which is making situations worse or preventing them from becoming better. When we are feeling badly about situations, we often want someone—in this case, the therapist—to tell us that we are fine and the world needs to change. However, that is not where the power is and it takes courage to face this reality."

It is hard to be a critic to ourselves. Yet once we brush off the often-surprising initial sense of rejection or harsh evaluation by others, there is a potential wealth of information there for us. I remember once criticizing a colleague, but he was having none of it. As a matter of fact, he went on to indicate that when he received my phone call criticizing him, he called others and asked them about me. After thinking to myself, "Me?" an important reality struck me: In every case, no matter what the motivation of the person offering criticism might be, there is good information to be mined *if* we have enough self-esteem and willingness to learn to mine it. In this case, I obviously was not the best person to be a prophet to him, but he certainly was waking me up to the lack of gentleness in my offering feedback. I needed to have a more tender, forgiving heart, like the one described in the following beautiful story from Jack Kornfield, in his book *After the Ecstasy, the Laundry*:

Many Japanese soldiers were stationed on islands throughout the Pacific during World II. As the Japanese pulled back, these islands were so quickly abandoned that when the war ended, there were still hundreds of loyal soldiers on duty who had no knowledge of their defeat. Over a few years most of these men were found and brought back by local people, but, as is common knowledge, a small number hidden in caves and forests continued to maintain their positions. They believed themselves to be good soldiers, trying to remain faithful to their country and defend the Japanese nation as best they could in the face of grave hardships.

One might wonder how these men were treated when they were finally found after ten or fifteen years. They were not considered misguided or fools. Instead, whenever one of these soldiers was located, the first contact was always made very carefully. Someone who had been a high-ranking Japanese officer during the war would take his old uniform and samurai sword out of the closet and take an old military boat to the area where the lost soldier had been sighted. The officer would walk through the jungle, calling out for the soldier until he was found. When they met, the officer, with tears in his eyes, would thank the soldier for his loyalty and courage in continuing to defend his country for so many years. Then he would ask him about his experiences, and welcome him back. Only after some time would the soldier gently be told that the war was over and his country was at peace again, so he would not have to fight anymore. When he reached home he would then be given an honorable welcome, celebrating his arduous struggle and his return to and reunion with his people.

We have judged ourselves and others for so long, carrying on over battle with the past, with life itself. In forgiveness we bow to it all with mercy and respect. . . . With forgiveness, our hearts become clear and whole for a time. The courage of our forgiveness frees us to enter the next step in our initiation [in the truth about ourselves and life.]

And, such a forgiveness for our past missteps is necessary if we are to be able to recognize and challenge the possibly comfortable, but not totally accurate, reputation we currently have with ourselves. This involves at its core finding and reclaiming key aspects of our narrative going forward—a process that is going to require patience, persistence and, yes, *courage*, at times.

THE UNRECOGNIZABLE YOU: ADDRESSING THE REPUTATION YOU CURRENTLY HAVE WITH YOURSELF

In order to untie the knot, you must first find out how the knot was tied.
—THE BUDDHA

There was no other voice like [poet] Edna St Vincent Millay's in America.
It was like the sound of an ax on fresh wood.
—LOUIS UNTERMEYER

You cannot, you cannot use someone else's fire. You can only use your own. And in order to do that, you must first be willing to believe that you have it.
—AUDRE LORDE, American writer, feminist and activist

I believed what I was told and not what my own eyes saw.
—MARGARET DRABBLE, English writer and critic

I n his book *Authentic,* Stephen Joseph sets out a challenge before us when he writes, "authenticity is not something that people either have or don't have. It is not like a qualification that you get, along with the certificate to hang on the wall. It is about the decisions you make in each and every moment and how you make them."

In Sidney Jouard's classic work, *The Transparent Self*, he recognizes the challenge of making such decisions when he writes, "Doubtless, when a person is behaving in ways that do violence to his integrity, warning signals are emitted. If only man could recognize these, diagnose them himself, and institute corrective action!" This requires an ability to attend to ourselves as a nonjudgmental listener, observer, or mentor would do.

Jouard adds to this, saying, "Self-disclosure is a factor in effective counseling or psychotherapy. Would it be too arbitrary to assume people come to need help because they have not disclosed themselves in some optimum degree to the people in their lives?" To this I would add full disclosure to *themselves* as well.

Jouard recognizes that it is necessary for people to play certain roles in society for it to function. Yet, what he emphasizes is that too often people see the role as equaling in some way the total self. This precipitates an obstacle to living completely, transparently, and in a way that does justice to the complete self or the original spirit that seems to drive it.

A healthy sense of self is essential for embracing our ordinariness. It is based on what William Appleton referred to as "the reputation you have with yourself." And so, two natural questions this proffers are: How did I get this reputation, and are the beliefs upon which it is based accurate?

Addressing these questions is crucial in discerning what is our true face. Our response to them can determine how we might lead the rest of our lives. If the questions remain unaddressed or unanswered, though, we may well end up journeying through life on automatic pilot dictated by un-examined and possibly inaccurate beliefs or unconscious "voices" from our past as well as early and present soci-etal dictates. They may not actually tell us the whole truth about ourselves but instead put us in a position to mimic others, rely too heavily on the reflection of self from those around us, or simply be the response to a desire to fit in with societal norms.

The result we risk may be a life in which our basic intuition about ourselves and our whole way of living lacks the peace and strength that should be ours when we are flowing with who we are. In such instances we might actually keep ourselves from taking our necessary place at the table of life and therefore prevent ourselves from being fully alive. Moreover, erroneous distorted or negative self-perceptions may interfere with our being full participants in fostering an accurate sense of self in others. Having an inaccurate self-image is a serious problem; it can have detrimental consequences of a social as well as per-sonal nature.

BASICALLY, HOW DID I ARRIVE
AT THE IMAGE OR SENSE I HAVE
OF MYSELF?

When we were very young we looked into the faces of our parents, day care workers, older siblings, and friends to see our reflection. Ideally, their eyes reflected their unconditional love and acceptance of us. This should then have encouraged our enthusiasm for life and helped us to see the loving face of goodness in the world around us. If so, we did not make our self-worth contingent on performance. Realistically, though, our parents and the significant others in our lives were "only human" and had needs of their own which were never completely met. They often came from situations that were far from perfect; the love and acceptance *they* received in their early years was not always unconditional. Without knowing it (or in the rare case that they were consciously trying to be malicious), our parents and the other significant people in our lives projected some of their own needs and demands onto us; because of this, their acceptance was conditional.

I was able to see this in one of my patients who was a child of survivors of the Holocaust. He was very talented, energetic, and creative. Yet he often chose partners who were not on his level, and he pushed people away because of his neediness. This behavior was partly due to the fact that from an early age he was being parented by persons who had been through the most horrible situation imaginable. They were in continual recovery and drawing from everyone around them to stay psychologically afloat themselves. This included their son, who was emotionally limping from carrying their burden from an early age without being fully aware of what was happening to him.

When any of us, including my patient to a more significant degree, introjects (takes into ourselves unconsciously) some of the self-esteem deficits our significant others might have had at the time, it makes matters more complicated. Because they were our guides, we followed them in ways that were rarely spoken about but which were subtly modeled by them and quickly learned by us. This mimicry became so imprinted that we may still follow them without knowing it. Here we find the truth of the saying "The apple doesn't fall far from the tree." After all, how many times have we said to ourselves, "I can't believe I'm doing this! My parents used to say this when I was a child, and I said I would never say such a thing or repeat this behavior."

The problem, then, is that we pick up styles of acting and negative or distorted messages about ourselves without even knowing it. These messages were frequently transmitted preverbally (even before we had mastery of spoken language), nonverbally, and indirectly. Thus, they are hard to uncover, evaluate, and correct, even if they are false. It is not unusual to hear people say, "I know I am a good person. I know I have many talents and people respect me. But when I do something wrong or someone says something negative about me, it seems to undo all the positives. I believe the negative comment represents how people *really* feel about me and what I really believe down deep to be true about myself." Such comments reveal a loyalty to some negative image of self, a self-defeating role or way of thinking learned early in life.

In most cases, unless we see what is happening, this negative "music" will continue to play in our minds. We will react and submit to it all our lives—often without even being aware of it. For, as Virginia Woolf noted in her essay, "Profession for Women," "It is far harder to kill a phantom than reality."

In some instances, the messages may be so distorted that a person needs psychotherapy to rework the early relationships he or she had. Michael Franz Basch discusses a view of famous self-psychology theorist Heinz Kohut in "Dynamic Psychotherapy and its Frustrations" which is related to this issue:

> What becomes a person's self-esteem—his sense of cohesion and worthwhileness—is developed through empathic transactions with his parents. When parents' empathy for their child fails significantly, the result is defensive behavior with which the child seeks to protect himself from further frustration, hurt, disappointment, overstimulation, and so on. These defenses and their offshoots, if not satisfactorily resolved, later form the problematic aspects of an individual's character. If that person becomes a [psychotherapy or counseling] patient he will sooner or later reenact in some fashion with the therapist the trauma of his earlier years, usually in response to a real or imagined failure in the therapist's

empathy. If the patient's subsequent defensive behavior is . . . recognized for what it is, its examination can lead to an understanding of the earlier struggle that the patient is unsuccessfully trying to resolve in the present.

Informal types of self-reflection; feedback from friends, family, and colleagues; as well as more structured interactions with therapists, counselors, mentors, coaches, or spiritual guides can be helpful ways of checking the accuracy of our view of ourselves. This is especially important with respect to the validity of any distorted or negative views we have of ourselves.

Such support can result in not only more accurate self-esteem and a healthy sense of self (ordinariness) but also a facility to be open to appropriate criticism and an ability to be a more genuine friend to others. We would also be strong enough to challenge societal and institutional structures when they oppress rather than enliven and empower all people.

The following story from Native America illustrates the importance of one's self-image and the potentially powerful impact of others' views of us. Having current positive, hopeful, and accurate reflections of self in terms of increasing the possibility of self-exploration, rather than letting our sense of self remain stagnant and distorted in some way, depends on this. The message of this beautiful story also reminds us of some of the basic themes of ordinariness (humility, simplicity, and a willingness to let go of a destructive self-image) that have been discussed thus far:

The Iroquois Indians tell a fascinating story of a strange and unusual figure they call "the Peacemaker." The Peacemaker came to a village where the Chief was known as "The-Man-Who-Kills-and-Eats-People." Now the Man-Who-Kills-and-Eats-People, the Chief, was in his wigwam. He had cut up his enemies and was cooking them in a massive pot in the center of the wigwam so that he might eat their flesh and absorb their mythical powers.

The Peacemaker climbed to the top of the wigwam and looked down through the smoke hole, say the Iroquois, and as he peered down through the smoke hole his face was reflected in the grease on the top of the pot. And the Man-Who-Kills-and-Eats-People looked into the pot, saw the reflection, and thought it to be his own face.

And he said, "Look at that. That's not the face of a man who kills his enemies and eats them. Look at the nobility. Look at the peace in that face. If that is my face, what am I doing carrying on this kind of life?"

And he seized the pot, dragged it from the fire, brought it outside, and poured it out on the ground. He then called the people and said, "I shall never again take the life of an enemy. I shall never again destroy or consume an enemy for I have discovered my true face. I have found out who I am."

And then, says the story, the Peacemaker came down from the top of the wigwam and embraced him and called him "Hiawatha."

Accurate Self-Appreciation and Space for Others to Thrive

From this story and the points made earlier, we can see some basic ways by which our self-image is formed, how it can have a serious impact on our self-esteem (what we believe and how we feel about our ordinary selves), and in turn how we will lead our lives. If we are able to see our "true face" reflected in the faces of those who love us unconditionally, we ultimately then feel the confidence to see our own errors and shortcomings in a different way. Instead of viewing them as "proofs" that we are bad, we see them as mistakes to be corrected or challenges to be taken on in life. The "positive paradox" is that with a healthy and accurate self-image, we are in a better position to honestly examine our errors, addictions, pettiness, cowardice, greed, anger, and other failings. People with a true sense and respect for their ordinariness don't measure self-worth by how they perform. Part of their humility is evidenced in their knowing that no one is perfect. Instead, in their enthusiasm for living compassionately, they seek each day to receive the welcoming spirit to be more responsive to what is good.

Given this, is it any wonder then that one of the most compassionate things we can actually do for others is to develop a clearer sense of ourselves—including our gifts? Or, in more colloquial terms, it makes sense that one of the greatest things we can do for others is to learn to like ourselves, to "get a kick" out of ourselves. This raises the possibility of their psychologically "catching" such an attitude themselves.

The reason why having this type of attitude is helpful to others (rather than merely being narcissistic) is clear if we think about it. People with solid self-esteem still feel the pain of rejection and failure, but they are less defensive, more able to deal with the anxiety, stress, and negativity of others, and are in a better position to inspire true hope during difficult times. As existentialist psychologist Rollo May points out, "high self-esteem doesn't protect us from self-doubts but it does enable us to entertain self-doubts without being devastated." The same can be said of people who embrace their ordinariness with a nonjudgmental but hopeful attitude of intrigue with respect to discovering their own "style."

Exploring the Unrecognizable You

The French philosopher Emmanuel Levinas, who is of Lithuanian descent, wrote a book-length essay entitled *Totality and Infinity*. His primary interest in it, and his entire philosophy, is the relationship of self and other. In Sarah Bakewell's book *At the Existential Café*, which was previously cited, the author shares the following experience Levinas had in a prison camp which shifted his thinking entirely. She writes:

> Like the other prisoners, he had got used to the guards treating them without respect as they worked, as if they were inhuman objects unworthy of fellow feeling. But each evening, as they were marched back behind the barbed-wire fence again, his work group would be greeted by a stray dog

who had somehow found its way inside the camp. The dog would bark and fling itself around with delight at seeing them, as dogs do. Through the dog's adoring eyes, the men were reminded each day of what it meant to be acknowledged by another being—to receive the basic recognition that one living creature grants to another.

In my own life, I have found that when I relax and am simply myself, subtle acceptance of self gets translated into respect for others. A key example of this was reflected in a surprising, memorable comment a patient made during a psychotherapy session long ago. We were coming to the end of the therapy and I commented on the progress she had made. After saying that, I asked her how she believed she had gotten to that point. My thinking in asking this question was that she would respond at length by reviewing what she had learned in therapy about herself. Instead, she said the answer to that question was quite *simple*. When she responded this way, I must confess this caught me off guard, so I followed up, asking, "Simple?" To which she replied, "Yes. When I came in to see you for my first session I simply watched how you sat with me and then I began sitting with myself in the same way."

Accurate self-esteem's development sometimes relies on the presence of another who provides an attitude of respect for who the person is rather than who we or others may want them to be. It can also reinforce what is unique about us and encourage us to tend to this gift as one would a flowering bush at the heart of a garden.

At one of the universities where I was on faculty I had the opportunity to have an informal meeting with its president just prior to the end of her tenure there. Just as we were wrapping up our discussion I decided I wanted to share with her my sense of gratitude for the talents she had, and I mentioned some of them by name.

When I finished, I could see that she was caught off guard. Then, after a brief pause, she smiled and responded, "Thank you for your kind words. In return, I'd like to mention one thing that has struck me about you. Despite all of your accomplishments, you have never lost that childlike passion for life and what is good."

Her comment as the president of this fine university, as well as her being a clinical psychologist herself and a person I truly respected, meant a lot to me. Not only because it was positive feedback but more so because of the talent she had focused on. The joy of being a boy at heart had always been something I valued and shared with others.

However, sometimes when I am this way, I say or do things without considering the timing or the person I am sharing it with. As a result, I hurt them, and if they share with me what I have done, it makes me sad in the moment as well. Sometimes this naturally leads to criticism of me, some of which can be hurtful.

All criticism is impure. Even if 99% is for good reasons, there is still that small piece of it that was not for mature or helpful reasons. When we offer it to others we feel we may be helping them become aware of an injustice done to us. However, even though this is true, it is a bit like old forms of chemotherapy in that it destroys the "good cells" as well. We not only provide helpful information; we hurt the good spirit that may be connected with it.

Since criticism is never pure, there is a temptation at times to condemn the messenger and say that the person is hurting us because of their own failings. While this is sometimes true to some extent, the danger is to simply blame the critic. Such projection of blame is very immature and helps no one. Another temptation is be too hard on ourselves in response to criticism. Rather than producing new learning, such personal attacks do nothing positive. And so, discouragement is yet a third temptation, since failings are often tied to the very gifts we have and it is easy to make the same mistake over and over again.

To the contrary, when criticism is received by us in the right way, it can provide several opportunities:

• Learning to be gracious in apologizing for the mistake and the hurt felt
• Being careful not to be over-responsible for the amount of upset experienced because there are a number of factors within the person offering the criticism

- Getting a chance to see more clearly where we need to "prune" our gifts so they are delivered in the right measure, at the right time, and with a clearer understanding of the relationship. Even if we do something with the best of intentions, if it is not done correctly it can cause harm.

The bottom line: If we drop a "verbal rock" on a person's head, on purpose or by mistake, the individual still gets a bump. No excuses. Just learning to do better and moving on is the answer.

Given this sense of the delicacy of criticism, another advantage of understanding criticism well is that we gain a better recognition of when and how to offer criticism of others. Knowing how criticism hurts me, it gives me pause as to whether I should offer it at all—and if so, how I should frame it—and to take a clear look at my own many motivations (i.e., seeking to find the impure ones that are certainly there as well as my "noble" ones) before offering or formulating my comments.

In a similar vein, when I am faithful to this, I find that I tend to give less nonessential feedback. Even when I do say something that I really feel will be of use, hopefully, I will frame it with a sense of understanding rather than indignant blame. In doing this, in receiving criticism myself, I must confess, I still don't feel any less sad at hearing how I have failed—even if I feel it is only in the other person's eyes. However, I am in a better position to encounter criticism as an opportunity to check and laugh at myself more, so I am more understanding of other people's reason to criticize and more careful in offering my own.

Will I fail others and myself again? Surely. Maybe I will catch myself a bit more quickly, though, and be a bit more forgiving of those who don't wish to see that critical feedback is not as cut and dry as it might seem. When we deal with it in ourselves carefully we can learn without injuring our own appropriate self-esteem. This is essential, as we don't want to diminish or, worse yet, eliminate the gifts we have in order to enjoy and share ourselves more freely with others.

I still remember a colleague sharing with me that she experienced a temptation to unduly temper the unbridled joy she had when conversing with others socially. When I asked her why she felt she should hold herself back, she said it was her husband's responses. She told me that sometimes he would react by non-verbally indicating she was getting too enthusiastic. He did this by motioning with his fingers as if they were legs walking off the table. After a while, she tamped down her spirit so much that he said she had stopped being fun anymore. Naturally, she responded to this with hurt and anger. If he had proffered his criticism in a good way and she had seen it as a sign to be a bit more aware of her style, which for the most part really was a great gift in interpersonal settings, all of this could have been avoided and her self-esteem strengthened rather than threatened.

The label "self-esteem" carries with it a lot of narcissistic baggage. And so, in a deeper fathoming of ordinariness, *true* self-respect and recognition are better routes to finding the reality about ourselves. Just as it is deceitful—and a setup for painful experiences later in life—to give every child a balloon for the same strength or talent even though they aren't equal in each child, it is misleading when we don't uncover and value the unique, different gifts each child actually has. This is especially true in the case of gifts that are overlooked or misunderstood.

Likewise, the need for accurate self-respect and recognition must be undertaken with us as adults as well. The persons who consult me often do so because of problems they are facing within themselves. While this is understandable, it is important that I not be trapped by solely seeing what they perceive as their lacks or errors to the point that I miss seeing their gifts.

At the very beginning of my training as a psychotherapist, one of my analytic supervisors at Hahnemann Medical College and Hospital set me on the right path in this regard. I had presented a person to him by outlining all the problems she was experiencing. He responded by telling me that I, indeed, had the psychopathology (problem issues) down pat, but he smiled in a rueful way and added, "While you did a splendid job presenting the person's challenges, if you leave it at that you will do all the work in therapy." When I asked him why this was so, his reply was quite simple: "Because you have not also elucidated the talents and gifts this person has which she will need to use to heal herself." This was an important teachable moment for me that affected how I worked as a therapist, coach, or mentor going forward. It also reminded me of how important such an insight was for how I viewed and treated myself.

People often come to me because they want to know what they are doing *wrong* or how their approach to a situation can be improved. Such an openness to altering behavior and looking at their cognitive style (ways of thinking, perceiving, and under-standing) is admirable. However, there is still a missing piece to the self-recognition equation if we collaborate only in looking at what is negative, dysfunctional, or lacking.

Even broader questions as to what we should be living for, while good, are misplaced if we don't know who we truly are. I find that when people come in for mentoring, coaching, therapy, or clinical supervision and they also want to under-stand themselves and their style a bit better, and find more peace in both their personal and professional lives, their situ-ation improves markedly. Instead of simply taking each day as it comes, they flow with their overall life in a more gentle, clear way. This is done in spite of the lures of so many other values that are not helpful and can cause undue confusion.

Ordinariness as a platform can have us look inward, rather than only for outside causes, to see how to live, what to em-brace, and what to reject. One of the challenges in doing this, of course, is over-involvement in, rather than freedom from, ourselves. Such freedom can be seen in how we work with or serve others. Peter Matthiessen notes this in his book *Dragon River*, about his journey in the Himalayas:

The Sherpas are alert for ways in which to be of use, yet are never insistent, far less servile; since they are paid to per-form a service, why not do it as well as possible? "Here, sir! I will wash the mud!" "I carry that, sir!" Yet their dignity is

unassailable, for the service is rendered for its own sake—
it is the task, not the employer that is served . . . to serve
in this selfless way is to be free . . . they are tolerant and
unjudgmental.

Writer Gertrude Stein was one of the persons Ernest
Hemingway turned to for advice on some of his early writing.
On one occasion, after reviewing it, her advice to him was to
"begin over again and concentrate." The same can be said of
the process of self-recognition of our own self-image. For instance, when we are able to concentrate with an eye to becoming
intrigued and challenged by what we are doing, without an
observing eye to see if we are successful or "good" at it in the
eyes of others, enjoyment and flowing with our lives become
more possible.

Once again, as Mathieu Ricard notes in his book *Happiness*,

> We can't all become Olympic javelin athletes, but we can all
> learn to throw the javelin and we can develop some ability
> to do so. You don't have to be Andre Agassi to love playing
> tennis, or Louis Armstrong to delight in playing a musical in-
> strument. In every sphere of human activity there are sources
> of inspiration whose perfection, far from discouraging us, in
> fact whets our enthusiasm by holding out an admirable vision
> of that to which we aspire.

He then adds, "Isn't that why the great artists, the men and
women of conviction, the heroes, are beloved and respected?"

Being Open to Letting Our Narrative Free

In some of my own previous writings (*Bounce, Perspective,* and *Night Call*) I have emphasized the importance of being open to changing our narrative. Some people who have broken through societal barriers express well the need to feel strongly if it is to happen.

A close friend of the poet Edna St Vincent Millay, Arthur Ficke, wrote to her after being struck by the originality of one of her poems. In Nancy Mitford's definitive biography of Millay, *Savage Beauty*, she shares a reflection on the interaction between the two of them about his reaction:

> Arthur was keen to understand just how Millay's poem had come into being, and he went about finding out just as a lawyer would—with innumerable probing and somewhat patronizing questions. Had she read Coleridge or William Blake? He asked, "How did you come by the image—'Washing my grave from me'? Did you *see* it, or was it a happy accident of composition, or did you get it from a book?"

According to her biographer, "That last [line] was nearly too much for Millay; she thought there were vastly few 'accidents of composition' than one might think." And so, Millay wrote back to Ficke, "As to the line you speak of—'Did you get it from a book?' Indeed! I'll slap your face. I never get anything from a book. I see things with my own eyes, just as if they were the first eyes that ever saw, and then I set about to tell, as best I can, just what I see." I think all of us should have the same kind of passion as Edna St Vincent Millay in viewing our own original style, but this would take an appreciation of the nuance of personality.

We often act as if our personality is like a town in which there are two sides of the track. On one side are our gifts and positive or signature strengths; on the other, our shortcomings and psychological defenses, lacks, or growing edges. In reality, they live side by side. In one of Henry James' most loved novels, *Washington Square*, one of the characters acclaims about another, "She's like a revolving lighthouse; pitch darkness alternating with a dazzling beauty." The same can probably be said, to a great extent, about many of us.

A major problem in our not seeing this is that we look at ourselves and others in ways that are not helpful. This is dramatically portrayed in the classic work of fiction *The Little Prince*, by Antoine de Exupery:

> Grown-ups love figures. When you tell them that you have made a new friend, they never ask you any questions about essential matters. They never say to you, "What does his voice sound like? What games does he love best? Does he collect butterflies?" Instead, they demand: "How old is he? How many brothers has he? How much does he weigh? How much money does his father make?" Only from these figures do they think they have learned anything about him.

If you were to say to the grown-ups: "I saw a beautiful house made of rosy brick, with geraniums in the windows and doves on the roof," they would not be able to get any idea of that house at all. You would have to say to them: "I saw a house that cost [a fortune]." They would then exclaim: "Oh, what a pretty house that is!"

Each person, including ourselves, has a style that is unique—even if the goals and philosophy of life are the same. This is illustrated quite well in a comparison of best friends contemplative writer Thomas Merton and the minimalist poet Robert Lax. Both men were struck by the way society was going in the 1940s and they wanted no part of it. They sought original, inspirational role models who were countercultural. In McGregor's book, *Pure Act: The Uncommon Life of Robert Lax*, McGregor notes this in the case of the Eastern spiritual figure, Bramacari. Lax was captured especially by the simple power of Bramacari's personality and attitude, what he referred to as "the kind of planet he came from." He added, "I had always felt there must be that kind of planet somewhere and I was glad to see a representative of it come our way at last."

Merton was also struck by this simple man dressed in bright robes and sneakers, who didn't eat meat but made no major point of that—he simply didn't eat meat. Nor did he wish to convert others to Eastern ways and encouraged those in the West to follow their own religion and spiritual leanings, but he did it in a deeper way—once again, not in his words but in the living of his life. He was a person who simultaneously modeled joy and spirituality, something that is often missing in various religions.

One of the unique contributions of McGregor's book is in pointing out that while both Merton and Lax were radical in their rejection of societal norms and in many ways followed the same star, *how* they sought out a different life varied markedly. Looking at them, you might ask yourself which one appeals to you more. For my part, I follow Merton's style, but now in my seventies I admire and seek to emulate more that of Lax. Their styles, forms of ordinariness, were—as McGregor reports—actually psychological bookends.

> [Lax] was more cautious than others perhaps, quicker to consider the consequences of things he did and learn from experience (his aunt said he was the only child who looked both ways before crossing a street in his baby carriage), but he lived a full social and physical life. . . .
>
> One of the main differences between Merton and Lax was that Merton was a brilliant and tireless self-promoter, while Lax was often taciturn or tongue-tied in public, relying on his work to speak for him. Another was that Merton was vitally concerned—in college and later—with finding answers, while Lax seemed much more comfortable with questions. Decades down the line, while Merton shouted to the world what he'd discovered in the cave of solitude, Lax sat quietly within, offering an occasional smoke signal. . . .

These [differing traits] were connected to decisive action in one and contentment to let life flow where it will in
the other. Lax told me once that whenever the two of them
went to a new place, Merton would set off immediately to
explore and get his bearings, while Lax would find a coffee
shop and contemplate the place from there. Merton was
physical and impetuous; Lax was awkward and slow to act.
Where the two met was in the thirst for understanding, their
desire to do good, their intelligence, and their humor. Even
here, though, they differed. Lax's tendency toward the simple
complemented and sometimes clashed with Merton's complicated thinking . . . [and] when difficulties arose, [Lax] slowed
down. He waited. He believed deeply in the adage that all
things come to those who waited. Merton forged ahead.

Another difference was that Merton was always concerned
that in seeking to learn about himself, he might become too
self-involved in the process. Lax felt none of this. In another
book about him, by Steve Georgiou, written more pointedly
on the spirituality of Lax (*Way of the Dreamcatcher*), Lax responds
to Georgiou 's question about whether he feels he completely
knows or is still trying to discover himself, in the following way:

> Honestly, I'm far from knowing myself completely. I keep
> trying to learn more, I really do. It would be good if I could
> discover more. There's so much left to see and hear. I'm al-
> ways listening to myself, looking within. I think that if we all
> try to discover more of ourselves, we can help each other out

in the understanding of who we are, both as individuals and as a collective people. Every day I come to see what makes me more peaceful. If I can find this out for myself, maybe my quest can eventually help others. There are so many points of connection between people, so many original sights and sounds that we share, as if we were one creation but didn't really know it, but maybe we were meant to find out slowly.

Later in the conversations with Georgiou, Lax would add, "I think it was the Taoists who said, 'If you relax and make yourself comfortable, you can journey anywhere.'" I think that was clearly his approach in a nutshell. Yet both he and Merton got along extremely well, mainly I think because they respected each other's ordinariness, style, and approach, even though it was so radically different from their own. This is certainly something for us to take from them: to seek to recognize and respect different styles and personalities, try to appreciate them in others as well as our own, and understand that each person has a gift that is both present and in development. As Zen master Shunryu Suzuki once noted to his disciples (I imagine with a twinkle in his eyes), "You are all perfect as you are . . . and you can all use a little improvement!"

Such improvement becomes more apt to take place when we observe ourselves nonjudgmentally so we can see as clearly as possible the style we have in place when we react to those our around us (in other words, have a greater sense of our temperament) and what elements of our style (e.g., helpful, easy going) seem positive and what are the challenging aspects of our style (e.g., judgmental, overly dependent).

Although ordinariness seems to be a fairly straightforward virtue to embrace, it can be a precarious undertaking at times. Looking at today's world of hype and narcissistic self-display, simply embracing our own ordinary self sometimes feels like standing in the middle of a field and seeing a summer storm quickly gathering in the distance. You can see a black wall of rain smoothly sweeping toward you, but you're not sure what to do.

Staying in the middle of the field is not safe if it is an electrical storm. And even if it isn't, you know by standing still you certainly will wind up getting soaked. Should you run for cover under a nearby tree? You might stay dry but if lightning hits the tree you may also end up dead. And if you seek protection in a safe place down the road, you might never make it in time to avoid being soaked by the rain. None of the options seem sensible or attractive.

Trying not to think about how we can further understand and express our ordinary self is certainly not the answer either. Yet, many of us feel we are at an impasse given how simply being yourself seems so countercultural in a world that is going in the other direction.

Somehow it seems more difficult than ever not to have the simple prizing and expression of our narrative be drowned out by the voices around us. At such times, the world may indeed seem to be a dark place to live—so much so that we even feel the "darkness" within us, in terms of our feeling alien, lost, and moving in another direction from where others seem to be happily going. The temptation at such points is to simply go along for the ride—even if it be someone else's and we know in our hearts that flowing with our own narrative might prove more deeply rewarding and freeing for us.

Rather than giving in to the natural tendencies to avoid the darkness that we are experiencing in our hearts and the world around us, facing it directly—possibly with the support of like-minded spirits—is of great value in embracing ordinariness. While we may not be able to prevent life's storm from chilling ourselves, we must do what we can if we want to create a fuller narrative. Included in this process is a willingness to uncover and face the unnecessary darkness we inadvertently may be producing in our own lives.

Unnecessary Darkness

The darkness we experience in life often tells just as much about us as it does about what we feel is its cause. In some cases, what it does reveal is that the darkness we encounter is really unnecessary if we are willing to be more honest and transparent with ourselves from the start.

Unfortunately, some of what we face that we find dark and difficult in appreciating and further becoming ourselves is of our own making. Yoda, the wisdom figure or "Jedi master," made this point in the movie *The Empire Strikes Back*, from the *Star Wars* trilogy that was popular in the 1980s and still remains of great interest today. In this movie, Yoda urges Luke Skywalker, the young man who is his disciple, to enter a cave that seems to emanate, danger, darkness, and produce fear. When young Luke asks Yoda what is in the cave, Yoda's simple response is: "Only what you bring in with you."

The same can be said of us when we take alonetime to reflect or meditate. Many thoughts and emotions will tear at us at times. Such interior factors, possibly set aside or ignored, include the following:

- Lack of true self-awareness, self-acceptance, and self-love
- Dishonesty with ourselves
- Intolerance of others
- Unfinished business with family and friends
- Suppressed or repressed negative feelings
- Poorly developed ethics, beliefs, and values
- Attachments or addictions
- Hidden, past, or unintegrated embarrassments
- Resistance to appropriate intimacy
- Failure to take care of oneself physically, psychologically, or spiritually
- Lack of honesty and openness during reflection, meditation, or in sharing with a mentor or therapist
- Lack of meaning in one's life
- Ungrieved losses
- Unacknowledged greed
- Unreasonable expectations of self and others
- A sense of entitlement in place of a spirit of gratitude

- Undealt-with anger, anxiety, and fear
- Unwillingness to risk and an inordinate need for unrealistic security
- Inability to experience quiet and solitude in one's life
- Unhealthy self-involvement or, at the other extreme, lack of healthy self-interest
- A failure or unwillingness to set priorities in life and then to live by them
- Irresponsibility
- Being overly perfectionistic and inordinately self-critical
- An unwillingness to accept love for who one really is except from certain individuals who are deemed essential to one's self-esteem
- Fear of responsibility and a tendency to project blame onto others

The darkness of a true encounter with self can be like looking in a very clean "psychological mirror" that crisply reflects those partially hidden and disguised parts of our personality that keep us chained to a view of self that isn't open and mature enough to unlearn and embrace new possibilities and truths. Instead, this mirror reflects what rigid defenses, personal immaturities, unresolved issues, hidden motivations, erroneous (yet thus far comfortable) self-definitions, and our chameleon-like behaviors. In essence, it confronts us with the darkness of our unintegrated self.

What, then, does this experience of darkness call us to do? I think it calls us to take steps to live life more authentically.

It invites us to shape a life where we can approach ourselves and others with a greater sense of honesty, clarity, and hope. It also calls us to be more psychologically responsible and clear. In seeking to be such a person, we emulate critical thinkers by asking such questions as:

- Am I willing to appreciate the ambiguity—the "gray areas"—of life rather than needing and seeking answers even in those areas where there are none to be had?
- Do I critique my attitudes, beliefs, and cognitions so that I don't slip into secure delusions or rest on past responses for current challenges?
- Am I slow to accept things rather than being subject to rhetoric or convenient conclusions about myself and others?
- Can I hold onto the possible as well as the probable without undue discomfort?
- Am I able to enter into the mystery of who I am instead of simply acquiescing to others' views of me or trying to find "psychological cookbook" approaches to self-understanding?
- Do I gravitate toward the quick solution or one side of an issue because I lack the courage and intellectual stamina necessary to have an open mind and an open heart?
- Am I so afraid of failure and rejection by others that I go along with what opinion I perceive as current rather than the ones that may lead me to a truer sense of who I am and could become with a bit more attention and effort?

- Am I truly open to a repeated conversion of my beliefs and attitudes, or do I resist the disturbing chill of the fresh air that must come in when I open my heart and mind's door to new information and ideas? More specifically, am I willing to examine unpleasant thoughts, impulses, and feeling so I can find out more about myself and the direction I am moving in life?[1]

Trying to be clear can be dangerous to the status quo, to our normal ways of thinking about ourselves and the world. This can be disturbing to both us and those around us. It can interrupt our automatic acceptance of so-called common sense and make us ask "Why?" and "Why not?" when others just go along almost without thinking about life, *their* life. When our thinking process is on "automatic pilot" we certainly cannot live who we are and might be. Instead, we allow the invisible puppeteers of habit and conditioning to take charge.

We can sometimes see this when a thinker or writer alters a saying that has drifted through the ages untested. This wakes us up to the fact that traditionalism, rather than a respect for tradition, is keeping some portion of ourselves back. Too often racism, ageism, sexism, and other types of prejudice designed to deflate ourselves and others' self-esteem is based on aphorisms that need to be turned upside down, and laughed about. Only then can we see that they contain the seeds of destruction of the ordinary self, not wisdom. Maybe that is what was behind the Zen-like adage (which I must confess I love) that the Australian social activist Irina Dunn created and wrote on a bathroom wall in 1970: "A woman without a man is like a fish without a bicycle."

And so, changing or expanding one's narrative means not simply believing the psychological stories or mental drawings others have made of us—even if they are partially true or even flattering. Our story is bigger and more complex than that. Yet, by taking some simple steps, our story can be opened up for possible redefinition. There are a number of ways we can do this, but essentially it involves activities that enhance new awareness, such as:

- Bringing to mind persons in your life that seemed to view you in a different or more positive light than others so you can be aware of and put into play behaviors and attitudes that have remained in the shadow of your life for some reason.

- Using imagery to encourage the practice of your less obvious traits. For example, if you are known as a listener (which is a wonderful trait), image yourself as initiating stories and comments in situations where you normally would have simply sat back and attended to what was going on around you.

- Being aware of those persons around you—even those who claim to have your best interests at heart—who provide negative responses to efforts on your part to highlight a different part of your style. Following this, call to mind positive experiences in your life (stamina, forgiveness, new initiative, acceptance) as well as those who reinforced them as a way to address the temptation to fall into a sea of shame rather than

confront even what you know to be "growing edges" in your personality that need to be addressed again and again.
- Balancing your own storylines by looking for styles of thinking and behaving that will balance out or prune your major way of interacting. So if you are an extrovert, look for times when you can listen, be reflective, or enjoy silent periods in solitude.

Such simple steps are designed to help in the exploration of the possibilities of one's ordinary self as one did earlier in life. According to famous developmental psychologist Erik Erickson, the task of adolescence is to create an identity for oneself. However, the task doesn't end there. To be clear about ourselves takes a great deal of energy and determination on our part. It will also require patience and perseverance and a tolerance for failure that we may not have at this point. Yet, such situations do not close the door on our becoming stronger now to embrace more fully our narrative. As a matter of fact, just as an experienced sea captain, learning from our mistakes and being interested in correcting them in the present can make us an even more apt explorer of the depth of our ordinary selves.

FOUR

Becoming "Sea-Kindly": Living with Greater Patience, Perseverance, and a Willingness to Fail

The most beautiful people we have known are those who have known defeat, known suffering, known struggle, known loss, and have found their way out of the depths. These persons have an appreciation, a sensitivity, and an understanding of life that fills them with compassion, gentleness, and a deep loving concern. Beautiful people do not just happen.

—Elizabeth Kübler-Ross

It takes more courage than we imagine to be perfectly simple with other men.

—Thomas Merton

She was, from the beginning, an original. Yet, she came to fear the power of her own originality, even as she made the most of it.

—Millicent Dillon, *A Little Original Sin: The Life and Work of Jane Bowles*

David Brazier, in his thought-provoking work *Zen Therapy*, writes:

We are born weeping and we die protesting. In between we hate getting older, getting sick, becoming tied up with circumstances we dislike, and being separated from the things we do like. We may even hate getting up in the morning. There is never a time when we are totally at ease. The body never feels completely comfortable from one minute to the next. Even more so the mind. Not only that but these bad states can have terrible consequences in the form of wars, persecutions, strife, competition, oppression and cruelty.

Later in this work, he builds on these comments by noting:

We also inwardly long for an answer, but, in most cases, we are unwilling to give up our kingdom. We have mastered many techniques for keeping our question bound and gagged. We coat our grit in plastic so as not to feel its sharp edges. Plastic does not work for long, however. The grit demands real pearl. The advance of life, again and again, inevitably exposes the inadequacy of our efforts to cover up the trouble inside.

These days, at such times, we are apt to seek out a therapist to, if I may change the metaphor, help us get the dragon back into the cave. Therapists of many schools will oblige in this, and we will thus be returned to what Freud called "ordinary unhappiness" and, temporarily, heave a sigh of relief, our repressions working smoothly once again. Zen, by contrast, offers dragon-riding lessons, for the few who are sufficiently intrepid.

Trudy Dixon said of Zen Roshi, Shunryu Suzuki: "The qualities of his life are extraordinary—buoyancy, vigor straightforwardness, simplicity, humility, serenity, joyousness, uncanny perspicacity . . . but in the end . . . it is the teacher's utter ordinariness. Because he is just himself, he is a mirror for his students. . . . In his presence we see our original face, and the extraordinariness we see is only our own true nature."

Yet, to be our ordinary self requires a sense of honesty akin to riding the dragon. Mounting the dragon requires patience, perseverance, and a willingness to fail. This outlook involves both great courage and a willingness to be authentic. It values remaining in touch with our real self and is best fostered by a milieu that enhances a trust that such genuineness will be accepted, encouraged, and embraced by a significant other in the past or the present.

With his emphasis on professional helpers using their own authenticity as part of the healing process, Sidney Jouard broke new ground in the mid-1960s with the publication of his book *The Transparent Self*. For me, it still remains an important work because of some of the key reflections that seem to recognize the importance and difficulty of embracing ordinariness. One such comment of his is as follows:

> A choice that confronts every one at every moment is this: Shall we permit our fellows to know us as we are now, or shall we remain enigmas, wishing to be seen as persons we are not? . . .

We camouflage our true being before others to protect ourselves against criticism or rejection. This protection comes at
a steep price. When we are not truly known by other people in
our lives, we are misunderstood. When we are misunderstood,
especially by family and friends, we join the "lonely crowd."
Worse, when we succeed in hiding our being from others,
we tend to lose touch with our real selves. This loss of self
contributes to illness in its myriad forms.

In writing this he is hypothesizing that a person, in his words,
"can attain to health and fullest personal development only in-
sofar as he gains courage to be himself with others and when he
finds goals that have meaning for him—including the reshaping
of society so it is fit for all to live and grow in."

In his early research he found that real self-disclosure
becomes more possible when one encounters an attitude steeped
in love and trust. Loving someone involves not only seeking to
be open but also putting in the energy to fathom the greater
totality of the other person.

However, he clearly recognizes that degree of disclosure
involves risk. Again, in Jouard's own words, "Loving is scary,
because when you permit yourself to be known, you expose
yourself not only to a lover's balm, but also to a hater's bombs!
When he knows you, he knows just where to plant them for
maximum effect."

Yet ordinariness, as in the case of self-disclosure, which relies
in turn on our being as aware as possible of our own complete

selves, is worth the courage and stamina it takes. And so we must set out on the path to ordinariness with both fortitude and appreciation for the rewards of being ourselves and opening the space for others to do likewise. Paul Hendrickson, in his book *Hemingway's Boat*, wrote, "There's a term old boatmen sometimes used to describe a reassuring boat in a heavy ocean: 'sea-kindly.'" Like such boats, people who value and live out of a spirit of ordinariness offer this assurance to the people around them. To reach an inner place where they can be clear, humble, and simple and claim their identity, they must also be willing to face fear and failure, to live with courage and patience.

It is unpleasant and painful at times to reflect on how we have failed. However, as French philosopher Camus notes, "When a man has learned—and not on paper—how to remain alone with his sufferings, how to overcome his longing to flee, then he has little left to learn."

There are a number of reasons that it is beneficial *not* to run away from life's dark psychological experiences—including those within us. Staying the course often results in freedom from the need for external approval. It also can result in the development of new insights and skills and a greater attention to our style. This helps us uncover signature strengths not previously observed or helped to mature. It can also lead to an understanding of those situations in which our very gifts can turn into problems for us, such as when our outgoing nature becomes attention getting when we feel undervalued by others. This whole process can bring us to an overall increase in both motivation and determination to see what can be fathomed when experiencing personal darkness. In other words, any suffering or pain encountered is not seen as the final word but possibly the beginning of new wisdom and greater freedom from egoism.

Over-concern with self-image can be a significant problem to those who wish to practice and enjoy the fruits of the virtue of ordinariness. Sometimes making light of such ego involvement is in order. For instance, the comedian Rodney Dangerfield years ago made a living out of telling self-deprecating jokes about himself:

When I was born, the doctor took one look at me . . . and slapped my mother!

. . . .

When I was interested in dating, I sent a letter and a photo to the lonely hearts club. They took one look at the photo and they said: We're lonely . . . but not that lonely!

. . . .

As a result of all this rejection, I went to see a doctor about psychoanalysis. After taking one look at me, he told me to lie down on the couch . . . face down!

. . . .

Aaron T. Beck, the founder of the cognitive-behavioral movement in psychotherapy, liked to tell these Dangerfield jokes to introduce his theory. He believed many of us attach meanings to a situation that results in our unnecessarily feeling badly about ourselves as persons. Honoring ordinariness, by contrast, allows us to see our place in life for what it actually is—something many of us wish to avoid even when we reach an age of maturity.

Psychologists have recognized this reality for many years, but the concept goes back eons before their discovery. Buddhist psychiatrist Mark Epstein writes in his book *Trauma in Everyday Life* that "[Buddha's] efforts were always in the service of re-leasing people from their fixed ideas about who or what they were, about freeing them from attachment to whatever concept they were clinging to, about loosening the hold that the fear-based ego claimed as its birthright."

To be relaxed with who you are, Epstein notes, is not easy, but the road through the tough patches of self-awareness cannot be avoided. In the words of anthropologist Pierre de Chardin, "It doesn't matter if the water is hot or cold if you have to walk through it anyway." And walk through it we must. In Epstein's words again, this time about himself:

> While comfortable in my academic world, I was uncomfort-able with myself. Deep down, I felt unsure. Not of my in-tellectual skills but of something more amorphous. I could frame it in terms of existential anxiety or even adolescent ennui, but it felt more personal than that. I was worried there was something wrong with me, and I longed to feel more at ease. I had the sense that I was living on the surface of myself, that I was keeping myself more two-dimensional than I really

was, that I was inhibited, or was inhibiting myself, in some ill-defined way.

In response, he reports that eventually in his work as well as in his life that "listening meditatively. . . . rather than . . . resisting the unpleasant noises and gravitating toward the mellifluous ones, we were listening in a simple and more open manner. We had to find and establish another point of reference to listen in this way, one that was outside the ego's usual territory of control . . . listening from a neutral place." In other words, he discovered an approach to transform the experience of "ground-lessness" into something "nourishing rather than frightening." He accomplished this through leaning back from what had formerly been filled with emotion and judgment, and this opened up the possibility for real involvement in and engagement with all the aspects of his personality and past.

From a personal standpoint, I have often found that three of the blind alleys of mindfulness are *arrogance*, where we seek to project the blame outward; *ignorance*, where we condemn ourselves, thinking this is the way to true knowledge; and *discouragement*, because we don't feel the progress, control, or success we have been taught to seek or it is not forthcoming as quickly or surely as we'd like. Instead, in seeking to understand who we are and live out of the freedom that is present when we appreciate more and more of the reality of ordinariness, we need a spirit of *intrigue*. With such a nonjudgmental energetic involvement in a search for the truth, we find the journey satisfying, no matter what we find.

In terms of trauma, which intensifies the challenges in the process of self-discovery and acceptance, Epstein adds that traumatic experiences are like "bits and pieces of catastrophe we dissociate from but still carry with us. . . . [They] are left hanging just outside awareness. They peek out from our dreams or nag at us in the privacy of our aloneness, a lurking sense of sorrow or disquiet that underlies our attempts to be 'normal,' but it is rare that we feel secure enough to let them speak." In quoting Michael Eigen, he notes further, "One has to learn to live with it, have a larger frame of reference, opening the playing field, making more room."

Returning home to our self is seen in sharp relief when viewing the journey of those traumatized when they were young. It is usually an arduous, lengthy process, and the dangers of being psychologically derailed for one's whole life is a real possibility for the traumatized. In the words of Maya Angelou, "There is nothing so tragic as a young cynic because the young cynic goes from knowing nothing to believing nothing."

Still, the challenges facing trauma survivors are of interest to us here because their dramatic passage from being the person they created because of the trauma to finding out who they might actually be is really a paradigm for all of us. In a way, everyone's journey toward embracing their ordinary self after undergoing the many strong influences from our environment requires facing to a greater or lesser degree at least some of the following situations:

- Experiencing negative emotions such as anxiety, depressive feelings, and difficulties in relationships
- Frustration, loneliness, guilt and shame, fear and regret, a sense of loss of the old self others have reinforced
- Persons in our environment uncomfortable with our changes
- A desire for the self that is familiar to others and an occasional pull back into previously "normal" ways of being part of society—even though such "normal" ways may be unhealthy

We can see this in the extreme in the case of certain persons who have undergone the trauma of sexual abuse. In attempting to integrate the abuse into their personal history but not be trapped by it in terms of present self-definition, a number of challenges must be faced on the road to acceptance of past realities. Otherwise, denial, avoidance, or surrender to a life defined by trauma is the result. In working with persons who have been abused, the therapist must aid them in integrating both unpleasant and pleasant memories of the past. In addition, the courage and stamina it took for the abused person to survive and recover needs to be brought to light and prized. In the process, they are also encouraged to accept parts of themselves that they perceive as weak or hurting while congratulating themselves for the movements toward change and embracing their ordinary selves.

This is not easy, because of fear, impatience, and the sometimes negative reactions of persons around the abused person
when that person begins to become free of the self that was
determined by the abuse and move into the self that is more
inclusive and not defined completely by the abuse. The anger
expressed at abusive behavior in the world as well as directed
at themselves may not receive the encouragement that it should
when it appears as a new style in a previously docile person. Yet,
reinforced it must be.

The journey toward recovery and reclaiming of the self
also exhibits wonderful new benefits. In discussions and life,
abuse becomes less of the focus. The person no longer focuses
so much on the past or is no longer inclined to portray themselves as a person without personal power; there is a lifting of
depression and a greater interest in the present and the future
than in the past. They also are more realistic. They don't continue to condemn themselves for what they had no control over
in the first place (not being able to resist, not coping as well
as they feel they "should" have, or not being able to outwit
the abuser). They are in the later process of healing instead of
merely having their grievances remain in a dormant state.

To a much lesser degree, there is the positive side to the psychological coin for those who have not been abused when they
also reclaim their ordinary selves that may have been detrimen-
tally conditioned by events and people in the past. In addition
to becoming freer to embrace one's talents and the joy of being

free to explore oneself further, feeling more at home in one's skin provides all of us an opportunity to

- Conserve energy, because we don't have to figure out which masks to wear for different audiences.
- Expand the frame of our narrative.
- Experience a sense of congruity and inner freedom in "simply" being ourselves.

To accomplish this, we need to take the time to view ourselves while seeking not to become overly involved in ourselves. We need the safety of good friends or mentors and a belief in self. And, we need to be aware of the different psychological portals, such as humility, simplicity, and others, through which we can view our ordinary selves in new, possibly creative ways. Accomplishing this requires pacing, a sense of intrigue about ourselves, and a willingness to take steps in new directions that can open up possibilities not previously chanced. But, above all, we need *patience* and *perseverance*. In her book *Leaving Before the Rain Comes*, writer Alexandra Fuller's shares that her father would call her on it when she had problems tolerating delay. He would say, "I always think it's worth remembering, tobacco's a fourteen-month crop." Whereas, with respect to the perseverance and resilience borne of maturity and perspective, her mother would note when she became unduly upset over something minor, "Save your tears for the big stuff."

From a poet's standpoint, Rilke put it this way, in a message of patience balanced by the need not to shy away from clarity, in the classic work, *Letters to a Young Poet*:

> Be patient toward all that is unsolved in your heart and to try to love *the questions themselves* like locked rooms and like books that are written in a very foreign tongue. Do not now seek the answers, which cannot be given you because you would not be able to live them. And the point is, to live everything. *Live* the questions now. Perhaps you will then gradually, without noticing it, live along some distant day into your answer. . . . Why do you want to shut out of your life any agitation, any pain, any melancholy, since you really do not know what these states are working upon you? . . . you must be patient as a sick man and confident as a convalescent; for perhaps you are both. And more: you are the doctor too, who has to watch over himself."

Yet, often our insecurities prevent us from being simply ourselves for others. A blind man once gave a eulogy for the famous Zen master Bankei. Included in it he said:

> Since I cannot see a person's face, I must judge his sincerity by his voice. Usually when I hear someone congratulate a friend on some success, I also hear envy in his voice, and when I hear expressions of condolence, I hear a secret tone of pleasure. Not so with Bankei; when he expressed happiness, his voice was completely happy, and when he expressed sadness, sadness was all I heard.

Martin Seligman and others, in a more research-based and comprehensive way, developed this style of self-appreciation and work with others, under the rubric "positive psychology." This is not simply sugar coating things or ignoring negative realities. It is a profound approach that appreciates with the same value the positive as it does the negative. Too often, psychology and society in general have valued the negative more and seen the positive as fluff. We need only watch television and see how the news is reported to see that society has jumped on the disease bandwagon.

And so, to help others and arrive at a stronger, more complete sense of self, we need to ask ourselves (as well as others) questions that will open us up. Such simple ones could include the following:

- What gifts do you feel you haven't explored and shared with others as fully as you would like?
- What obstacles to embracing your own sense of ordinariness or wholeness do you feel are part of your resistance to letting go, opening up, and embracing more of who you might be?
- In what way have you found that your own darkness or the suffering of other people has enabled you to be more grateful for what you have in your life that is wonderful?
- What are some recent experiences or ways of viewing yourself that you felt broadened your sense of self?
- In looking over your life, what events have made you value your own life differently and more deeply?

- What words would you like written on your epitaph, and how might you practice them more fully at this point than you might have been able to when you were younger?
- Given your sense of self, what is the "mission" you have had in your life up to this point—even if it hasn't been seen from this frame of reference—and how would you like it to change now?[1]

A fuller understanding of the primary balancing talent we have (as well as the other less developed ones) enables our awareness to become richer for ourselves as well as those in our family, our circle of friends, and others who encounter us. Such clarity also helps us avoid being novelists about our lives, where we mix fiction with reality to make our sense of self in our own mind more appealing, fascinating, or aboding.

Fathoming all our gifts, small and large, allows the reality of our total self to be enough. In such a position, we are "extra-ordinary" and know this is wondrous in and of itself. In turn, it allows us to help others explore their sense of self with a greater sense of intrigue and wonder. Yet sometimes this requires that we turn to others who can walk with us as "mentors in ordinariness." While they are in a position to gain greater clarity as to what may be obscure to us or hurtful to others in the way we deal with them, they can also help us to keep our own sometimes harsh self-appraisal in balance. In addition, they can guide us to keep the criticism we receive from others in perspective, as the following story from

Benjamin Hoff does, in his book *The Te of Piglet*, which is a favorite of mine:

> While traveling separately through the countryside late one afternoon, a Hindu, a Rabbi, and a Critic were caught in the same area by a terrific thunderstorm. They sought shelter at a nearby farmhouse.
>
> "That storm will be raging for hours," the farmer told them. "You'd better stay here for the night. The problem is, there's only room enough for two of you. One of you will have to sleep in the barn."
>
> "I'll be the one," said the Hindu. "A little hardship is nothing to me." He went out to the barn.
>
> A few minutes later there was a knock on the door. It was the Hindu. "I'm sorry," he told the others, "but there is a cow in the barn. According to my religion, cows are sacred, and one must not intrude on their space."
>
> "Don't worry," said the Rabbi. "Make yourself comfortable here. I'll go sleep in the barn." He went out to the barn.
>
> A few minutes later there was a knock at the door. It was the Rabbi. "I hate to be a bother," he said, "but there is a pig in the barn. I wouldn't feel comfortable sharing my sleeping quarters with a pig."
>
> "Oh, all right," said the Critic. "I'll go sleep in the barn." He went out to the barn.
>
> A few minutes later, there was a knock at the door. It was the cow and the pig.

Whether we like it or not, in the end, we are the ones who have the main responsibility for the definition of ourselves and whether we can live a truly mature adult life, which includes letting go of outmoded and erroneous (though familiar) self-definitions. As professionals from the reality (now choice) therapy school of thought would point out: We must be willing to recognize, understand, accept, and live within the "givens." Or, as Kahlil Gibran, in his famous work *Sand and Foam*, wrote: "We choose our joys and sorrows long before we experience them."

The fact that we are provided with limits and "givens" in our life is a reality. To deny such constraints would be "Pollyannish" in our thinking. Still, despite these natural constraints, there is much more before us—both in the present moment and in potentiality—that we are missing because of our unwillingness to let go of consciously and unconsciously, innocently and maliciously, definitions that are imposed on us. I think former Secretary General of the United Nations, Dag Hammarskjöld, was correct when he said, "We are not permitted to choose the frame of our destiny. But what we put into it is ours." What often holds us back in this respect are unnecessary fears, an inability to face or navigate failure, and a resistance to openness and change.

Fear is part of life. Mark Twain, in his 1894 work, *Pudd'nhead Wilson*, wrote, "Courage is resistance to fear, mastery of fear, not absence of fear." Twain was very conscious of what holds us back because he put such a high value on "discovery." In *Innocents Abroad* he wrote:

What is it that confers the noblest delight? What is that which swells a man's breast with pride above that which any experience can bring to him? Discovery! To know that you are walking where none others have walked; that you are beholding what human eye has not seen before; that you are breathing a virgin atmosphere. To give birth to an idea—to discover a great thought.

Nowhere is such discovery more profound on this earth, I think, than within oneself. Whereas a sense of ordinariness sets the stage for this, fear that blossoms because of egoism and an environment that is toxic, or at the very least not very generative, stymies such uncovering and discovery. And so, how we deal with failure and fear is part of the search for the full expression of our ordinary self.

DEALING WITH FAILURE

In her article, "Learning to Fail,"[2] Jessica Bennett reports on programs being initiated at Smith College to help students who were high achievers in high school cope with the setbacks that come with being part of a pack of other outstanding minds. One creative way this was done was projecting onto a large screen on campus during finals week the following admissions of failures by peers and instructors:

"I failed my first college writing exam," one student revealed.

"I failed out of college," a popular English professor wrote. "Sophomore year. Flat-out, whole semester of F's on the transcript, bombed out, washed out, flunked out."

One of the goals in doing this was to teach those who are referred to at Harvard as "failure deprived" an appreciation of the reality that failure is part of learning. It is part of reaching for the highest levels. Such an awareness helps destigmatize failure and thus enhances resiliency. The reality is that, statistically, the more we are involved, the more we increase the chance for failure, so we need to know how to deal with it and benefit from it.

Once when I presented a lecture on involvement, spontaneity, and being a gentle, ordinary presence in the world, during the question-and-answer period, one person ventured to say, "You make being a sensitive, ordinary person sound so positive. But I have this fearful question nagging me. What if I fail?"

To which I responded, "Oh, don't worry about that. Let me assure you. You *will* fail!"

At this her eyes opened wide, she made a face, and said, "Oh, great! Thanks!" and this brought laughter to all present—including the two of us. Yet, as Albert Einstein is once reported to have quipped, "Anyone who has never made a mistake has never tried anything new." This includes the way we view ourselves.

The reality is that attempting to simply be ourselves and be open to who we are more fully at each stage of life brings with it a certain amount of failure. Part of this failure which often hurts us the most is the recognition (or resistance to such an awareness) of the personal limits, poor motivations, and personal inadequacies we may have partially hidden from ourselves or feared looking at up to this point.

In my case, for example, I have always thought of myself as a generous person who has a hard time setting limits with people. But over the years I have come to see more and more that instead of being true to myself and others, the reality is that at times I am a fake. One reason for this is that I like to look good, and because of this often promise more than I can realistically deliver. Then when people call on me to deliver, I pull back and think to myself that they are asking too much.

On the other hand, if I were willing to know and embrace myself better, I could provide a more realistic welcome to others, prevent hurt on their part, and also head off the sadness I feel when people are angry or upset with me because I have let them down. And so the questions I must face continually are: Am willing to give up being a showman in friendship I offer people but sometimes I don't really mean? Am I also willing to recognize the hurt that bravado and false generosity (sometimes alcohol-induced) can produce?

As you can imagine, it's not so easy for me to have such truthful eyes. I guess it isn't for anyone who wants to be an honest person without guile who can love in a concrete and real way. Abstract love never involves risk or failure, just good wishes and a rich imagination. Still, love in the concrete often is not pretty, but its results are wonderful if we are willing to take the chance to encounter ourselves honestly as we open ourselves to others in ways that reflect our ordinary selves.

Failure provides helpful information with respect to uncovering egoism, the need for new approaches to ourselves and life, the need for further mentoring in certain areas, important understanding of our expectations, and insight into what we are especially sensitive about and why this is so. However, carefully mining our failures is often difficult because of a tendency in many of us toward self-condemnation or projecting the blame as a way of avoiding being pulled down by self-awareness of our mistakes or shortcomings.

One way we can face this, as well as strengthen our ability to readily appreciate our gifts and recognize our foibles, is when we can gently laugh at ourselves. When people enjoy themselves and can get in touch with their own natural inner beauty, they are in the strongest position to tease themselves in good ways. Humor frees us to be more open to others instead of being overly protective due to unnecessary problems with our public image. As a result, when we are comfortable with, and knowledgeable about, both our gifts and growing edges, we can relax with ourselves. When we feel this way, as has been previously emphasized, it is not then just about us, because we can enable those around us to relax with themselves as well.

In my travels I have found this to be so, not simply with individuals but also with certain cultures. It is almost as if they know what others are saying about them is true to an extent, and rather than covering it over they tease about it. I have particularly recognized this in Newfoundlanders, and I respect them for their self-awareness and humor.

In Canada, people in most of the provinces tease about persons from Newfoundland. Other Canadians speak about Newfoundlanders' simplicity and country-like ways with a twinkle in their eyes, because they know they lack the transparency and simple nature of many people from this province. The Newfoundlanders know that this is said of them. Yet, rather than trying to deny or cover it up, they embrace it with good fun. As a result, when you are with them, it frees you up to be yourself as well. I know this from experience.

On my first visit to Newfoundland I was there to do some consultant work and present a few lectures on resilience. After my visit, I boarded a flight to Nova Scotia for a connection into the United States. I had just taken my seat when a fellow literally plopped into the seat next to me, quickly leaned over in my direction, and asked, "Are you from Newfoundland? Are you a Newfee?" "No," I said, "I'm not." After I responded in the negative, he quickly followed with the question, "Well then, do you know where the Newfees keep their armies?" "No, I said." To this he replied, "Up their sleevies!" Making a face and laughing I retorted, "We're not going to do this for the whole flight are we?"

Then, just after that, a really chipper old fellow from one of the French areas of Newfoundland who was sitting three rows in front of us pulled down his fiddle from the overhead rack and started to sing and play. What a flight it was! What wonderful people Newfoundlanders are. I love them. Their joy and ability to poke fun at their own sense of simplicity made me more easily relax, accept more my own ordinariness, and better feel a sense of joy that was deep within me.

It's wonderful when we can laugh at ourselves, our dark side, and our foibles. Without such an ability to do so, there is a tendency to bury our negative style through denial or bravado. When we do, we harm our ability to be self-aware and ordinary and, in turn, increase our defensiveness with others while enveloping ourselves more completely in a cognitive envelope of egoism.

Honoring our ordinariness and having a sense of humor go well together. They set the stage for us to relax enough to see ourselves honestly, not to take ourselves too seriously, and to learn how we can best be a welcoming presence to others without unduly carrying the burden of our pride. The joy of being at ease with oneself is a great and gentle gift. Without it our presence to others becomes just another chore, rather than a wonder to experience even in the darkest of times.

ENCOUNTERING FEAR

Fear of what would happen if we let go and were simply ourselves is another reason why we might avoid exploring and experimenting in the search for the ordinary self. Pema Chödrön puts it well, in what has become a contemporary classic for many in the Buddhist tradition, *When Things Fall Apart*, when she addresses both the desire and fear one encounters in moving closer to the truth about aspects of oneself:

> Embarking on the spiritual journey is like getting into a very small boat and setting out on the ocean in search for unknown lands. With wholehearted practice comes inspiration, but sooner or later we will also encounter fear. For all we know, when we get to the horizon, we are going to drop off the edge of the world. Like all explorers, we are drawn to discover what's waiting out there without knowing yet if we have the courage to face it.

She goes on to encourage us to "stay with the shakiness" that certain encounters leave us with. She aptly notes, "Curiously enough, if we primarily try to shield ourselves from discomfort, we suffer. Yet when we don't close off and we let our hearts break, we discover our kinship with all beings." The "advantages" of not being self-aware and seeing the process of fuller self-discovery as an ongoing process that never ends can be very costly to us. And so, in lieu of whatever comfort remaining oblivious of how we have given up our own selves and have traded habit for personal dynamism because of fear, the fear must be confronted directly. As a matter of fact, in staring our fears in the face, we may be shocked at how easily they melt and a new willingness to be grateful for the opportunity to change arises. The interpersonal environment we had early in life and we are in now often operates on fear. As highlighted at other points in this book, fear is often sold to us when the danger is not there but is being exported to us for other reasons.

Fear is often misplaced, even on a larger screen. We worry about things we needn't. In a chapter aptly titled "There's Never Been a Better Time to Be Alive," in his book, *The Science of Fear*, Daniel Gardner writes:

> There are clouds on humanity's horizons, of course. If, for example, obesity turns out to be as damaging as many researchers believe it to be, and if obesity rates keep rising in rich countries, it could undermine a great deal of progress. But potential problems like this have to be kept in perspective. "You can only start worrying about overeating when you stop worrying about undereating, and for most of our history we worried about undereating," [economic historian Robert] Fogel wryly observes. Whatever challenges we face, it remains indisputably true that those living in the developed world are the safest, healthiest, and richest humans who ever lived. We are still mortal and there are many things that can kill us. Sometimes we should worry. Sometimes we should even be afraid. But we should always remember how very lucky we are to be alive *now*.

Gardner then goes on to note that fear is a marketing tactic. People make money from enhancing our sense of insecurity and needs, even though we are living in a first-world nation where starvation is less of an issue than obesity is. The same can be said of the goals of advertising with respect to ordinariness. We are lured to be more concerned with the niceties of life, as if they were true needs, than the true essentials—not only in the case of things but in the case of our identity.

Knowing this, Thomas Merton wrote in the following passage from his novel, *Argument with the Gestapo*: "If you want to identify me, ask me not where I live, or what I like to eat, or how I comb my hair, but ask me what I am living for, in detail, and ask me what is preventing me from living fully for the thing I want to live for." I think this is a question we need to be mindful of ourselves, especially when we can sense we are taking ourselves too seriously or becoming upset that others aren't honoring us as we feel they should. It is also a question worth exploring with mentors who model ordinariness for us in its fullest form. When we do this, we will be in a better position to receive good feedback and support. In addition, the learning and example provided will help us, in turn, to model it for others in our actions as well as in the feedback we give them when they request it.

FIVE

Mentors in Ordinariness: Experiencing Authenticity in Practice

She would go into people's lives and make some dormant thing inside come to life.[1]
—Robert Faulkner, comment about writer Jane Bowles

"Mr. Norris acted like I was the most important girl in the world," she said.
"You were. That was Gene's secret.
All of us were."
—Pat Conroy, *The Reading Life*

In everyone's life, at some time, our inner fire goes out. It is then burst into flame by an encounter with another human being. We should all be thankful for these people who rekindle our inner spirit.
—Albert Schweitzer, physician, missionary, scholar

In confronting a young man who she was fond of but who was not responsive in the way she had hoped, poet Edna St Vincent Millay said, "There is no shelter in you anywhere." The exact opposite of this is "the mentor of ordinariness" who is present to us in ways that awake, support, inspire, and enable a healthier perspective. Such a guide truly believes in the Cameroonian proverb:

> *If you wish to go fast, go alone.*
> *If you wish to go far, go together.*

Zen master Shunryu Suzuki advised those seeking a mentor or spiritual guide to seek to meet someone as sincere as themselves.[2] I think all of us have experienced a peaceful sense of ordinariness with certain people. I remember visiting someone who was so real, nondefensive, accepting, and self-aware that during the visit I felt no stress or anxiety at all. I could be myself; it was enough. I even had the strange sensation after I left him that I had not aged while in his presence! After all, how could I? There was no pressure when I was with him. As I walked away, I recalled the words of Peig Sayers, who lived in the Blasket Islands off the coast of Ireland. The winds were so violent there was not even a large tree that had endured. When asked how she and others lived there, she responded: "It is in the shelter of each other that the people live."

Psychotherapy should be like this. As Brazier notes, "The safe space of therapy depends upon the therapist's calm. As therapy progresses, the client too becomes calmer. Tranquility erodes the mind's conditioning. Conditioning makes us compulsive. . . . The person whose life is governed by 'I could not possibly . . . ' 'I must never . . . ' 'I always have to . . . ' and so on, is not free and feels inwardly oppressed." In contrast, as

Brazier states later in *Zen Therapy*, "the therapist models stillness and is not frightened by the client nor what they present. The client feels driven, but the therapist demonstrates that this is not inevitable. The therapist shows that she can hear what the client has said and is not panicked by it. Being inwardly still, the therapist is able to listen without reacting or jumping to conclusions."

Truly ordinary people, in whom we can sense trust in and acceptance of us as well as the inner calm Brazier speaks about, also have a way of awakening us to recognize our deep-seated pride and biases. This is revealed in a striking way by Harvard psychiatrist Robert Coles' encounter with Dorothy Day, the co-founder of the Catholic Worker movement, that he shared in his book, *A Radical Devotion*:

> It was on an afternoon, almost thirty-five years ago, that I first met Dorothy Day. She was sitting at a table, talking with a woman who was I quickly realized, quite drunk, yet determined to carry on a conversation. The woman . . . had a large purple-red birthmark along the right side of her forehead. She kept touching it as she uttered one exclamatory remark after another, none of which seemed to get the slightest rise from the person sitting opposite her.
>
> I found myself increasingly confused by what seemed to be an interminable, essentially absurd exchange taking place between two middle-aged women. When would it end— the alcoholic ranting and the silent nodding, occasionally

interrupted by a brief question, which only served, maddeningly, to wind up the already overtalkative one rather than wind her down? Finally silence fell upon the room. Dorothy Day asked the woman if she would mind an interruption. She got up and came over to me. She said, "Are you waiting to talk with one of us?"

One of us: with those three words she had cut through layers of self-importance, a lifetime of bourgeois privilege, and scraped the hard bone of pride: "Vanity of vanities; all is vanity." With those three words, so quietly and politely spoken, she had indirectly told me what the Catholic Worker Movement is all about and what she herself was like.

Maybe truly ordinary individuals can be like this because they don't base their self-esteem on a distorted, narcissistic belief in their own accomplishments or image. They're not busy worrying about losing what they don't need. Consequently, they can be less defensive and more welcoming.

Another example of this type of attitude is contained in a vignette related in *My Favorite Questions* by Norman Vincent Peale about the renowned evangelist, Billy Graham:

During one of the [Graham] crusades in London, the British newspapers quoted some cutting remarks about him by a well-known clergyman of that country. It was reported that when someone began telling Billy about this he said: "God bless that man. If I were in his place, I'd probably feel the same way about me."

Peale notes how "such an attitude ensures personal peace of mind as well as the love and respect of other people. If only we could be that way more of the time."

In a similar vein, Sandy Johnson, in her volume *The Book of Tibetan Elders*, wrote, "I had heard the Dalai Lama described as an emanation of the Buddha of Compassion, a god-king, a living deity of boundless love and compassion—descriptions that have only limited meaning to a person who is not a Buddhist. Sitting across from me was a man of such ordinariness, such unself-consciousness, a man so open and simple that one forgets what has been written."

Yet, the ordinariness of which Johnson—as well as many others who have met the Dalai Lama—speaks is partly the result of an intentional effort on his part. In his own words, recorded in *The Book of Joy*, he states,

> When I meet someone . . . I always try to relate to the person on the basic human level. . . . That way, there is in fact no need for an introduction. If on the other hand, I relate to others from the perspective of myself as someone different— a Buddhist, a Tibetan, and so on—I will then create walls to keep me apart from others. And if I relate to others, thinking that I am the Dalai Lama, I will create the basis for my own separation and loneliness. After all, there is only one Dalai Lama in the entire world. In contrast, if I see myself primarily in terms of myself as a fellow human, I will then have more than seven billion people who I can feel deep

connection with. And this is wonderful, isn't it? What do you need to fear or worry about when you have seven billion other people who are with you?

Reading this, I am not surprised to read Sandy Johnson's words about the Dalai Lama being a man of such openness and simplicity. Those are the core traits of a mentor in ordinariness.

In the search for our ordinary selves, we often find it necessary to enlist the help of others who have already done the work necessary to "simply" find and be themselves. Such mentors or wise figures don't ask us to impersonate them but instead to have the patience and courage, as previously discussed, to find our own map to explore our ordinary selves.

For many, ordinariness seems an unnecessary or too difficult option. They are comfortable enough wearing other people's clothes. Yet there are some who, like adopted children interested in meeting their birth parents, want to fathom more of who they are and might be given more knowledge and space for development. For such persons desiring to live out of a more genuine and congruent life takes effort. As in the case of learning to play a musical instrument, honoring the process involves more, much more. As Russian-born American pianist and composer Vladimir Horowitz noted and which I feel provides a good metaphor for the journey to more fully embrace ordinariness, "The piano is the easiest instrument to play but the hardest instrument to play well."

Given the difficulty and nuances in such a journey some-times it is necessary to make it in the company of other wiser travelers. In the words of Reinhold Niebuhr, "Nothing we do, however virtuous can be accomplished alone."

In a broader sense, we are fortunate if the community in which we place ourselves or are placed is committed to helping us face or circumvent obstacles to ordinariness. Just as the space of alonetime enables us to become clearer, so does the right in-terpersonal network. For my part, I have always suggested that there be four voices in it: *the prophet,* who asks us, "What voices are guiding you?"; *the cheerleader,* who is sympathetic and sup-portive during dark times; *the harasser/teaser,* who helps us avoid taking ourselves too seriously while being serious in our intent to be ordinary; and *the inspirational voice/friend,* who calls us to be all that we can be without embarrassing us that we are where we are at this point in life.

Sometimes mentors also use spontaneous events or humor to help people recognize that the journey to ordinariness is through gaining one's own perceptual clarity, even though it is facilitated by another. In his classic work, *Journey in Ladakh,* Andrew Harvey shares an example of this.

> We woke before dawn, washed in icy water, went down
> to the prayer room for morning prayers. The Rinpoche was
> amused that I had stayed the night. After prayers he waved me
> to him and said, "So you have decided to stay with us?"
> "I wish I could."

"You can stay as long as you like. Come when you like and go when you want."

I bowed my head to thank him and my glasses fell off into his hands. He laughed and laughed and waved my glasses in the air, and then put them with a great air of conspiracy into his yellow silk shirt.

"I am going to keep them for myself," he said.

"You can keep them, of course. But I wish," I said, "you would give me back your eyes instead. You can keep mine as long as you like."

He put my glasses back on with his own hands.

"No. You must see with *your* eyes, not mine. Perhaps I can help you to see with your eyes."

"If you could help me to see with my eyes, I would be grateful to you."

"I do not want gratitude. I want you to stay a little time with us, to come when you want and learn what you need. That is all."

True mentors in ordinariness welcome people in a very un-pretentious way. Steve Georgiou, in his book *The Way of the Dreamcatcher*, states that his mentor, Robert Lax, greeted people in a way that made them feel accepted and encouraged and that

he looked at them with a kind of happy awe, as if hailing a company of saints. He addressed his audience with kindness and focused on them completely, carefully, honestly, and with genuine love . . . those who left him broke into warm and carefree smiles. . . . As might be expected of a reclusive, dedicated contemplative, Lax did not talk much, nor did he desire manifold attention. Instead he preferred to maintain a low profile and listened intently, using his own silence to draw ideas out of others.

Peter France, in his book on the Greek island of Patmos, referred to this welcoming spirit in a unique way. He also emphasized that all of us should not only admire it as rare—which it unfortunately is today—but that we should emulate it. He wrote:

> In fact, "nice guys" on Patmos—and the phrase, of course, includes both sexes—are recognized by everyone and even labeled as such. They have a quality that is called *charis*. The dictionary defines the word as "charm" or "grace." It does exist elsewhere, but rarely. Here on the island you might find it in the baker, the dustman, a priest, a schoolteacher—I have seen it in all of them—and you recognize it immediately. It shows first in the eyes. They are calm, steady, mild, full of interest but without aggression. The person with *charis* has humility in the sense that the Desert Fathers understood it: not as an ingratiating meekness but as a keen interest and enthusiasm for the other person. It has to be admitted that sometimes people with *charis* do come in last. But that is not a law of our society. On Patmos, those who have finished first are respected for not flaunting it.

In looking for a mentor, when I first sought ongoing guidance to further discover and become who I might be with a little more clarity and support, I sought someone who reflected the following type of traits:

- Was able to balance gentleness with clarity in the questions asked of me—especially those that touched on areas about which I was unsure, defensive, or sensitive
- Provided the setting for me to experiment with new thinking and to find essential truths upon which to base my life more securely
- Demonstrated faith in me even when I failed and resisted insight and change
- Provided the psychological space to "speak to think" rather than feel everything I said had to be thoroughly thought out first
- Encouraged me to be myself and not fear rejection or ridicule
- Helped me recognize that it was not the amount of darkness in the world or me that mattered but how I stood in the darkness with as healthy a perspective as possible
- Did not ask me to emulate the person mentoring me but to have his sense of ordinariness give me the courage to "simply" be myself
- Offered a broad approach to searching further when I was lost so that I wasn't given someone else's answers but provided the tools to find my own

• Had the sensitivity to appreciate my sense of "lostness" when it occurred and appreciate my mood as well as my words, my uncertainties as well as what I felt I knew

Added to these qualities are the expectations we have of a true friend. Stephen Joseph, in his book *Authentic*, offers expectations of genuine friends, which he introduces with three questions:

Do I expect others to be genuine with me? Do you put up with lies and half-truths from your friends? Do you sometimes feel like you are their back-up plan? Raise your expectations and put your energy into those relationships that are genuine and truly respectful of you.

Do I expect my friends to be unconditional with me? Do you ever feel that your friends only love you if you are the person that they want you to be? Friends should love you just as you are and be pleased when good things happen to you.

Do I expect my friends to be interested in and caring of me? Do you feel that your friends try to see things from your point of view? Or do they try to convince you to see things in the same way they do? Friends should cherish you and how you see things.

In his book on Menachim Mendel Schneerson, *Rebbe*, author Joseph Telushkin writes: "Chasidim trust a Rebbe's advice on such a variety of issues because they feel a Rebbe, in addition to having wisdom, has achieved a spiritual level of *bittul ha-yesh*, a nullification of his personal will. Such a person, one

who can negate his own ego before God, and who can negate his own ego in the presence of others, becomes a pure
vessel for transmitting God's wisdom." Rabbi Salman Posner, a
contemporary Chasidic philosopher, Teluskin then shares, also
expresses a similar sentiment, noting that "the Chasid is certain that the Rebbe is selfless enough to tell him not what the
Rebbe might personally prefer, but only what the Torah would
have the Rebbe say."

In reflecting on Telushkin's view of a rebbe and in reviewing
this list, I recall a woman who was not Jewish referring to her
mentor in a way that made me want to search and find one myself. She said that out of his many gifts, in the end it was her
teacher's utter ordinariness that she found most impressive. She
felt that it provided a psychological mirror to help her unearth
and claim her own. This point brought to mind a comment
Jack Kornfield made in his book, *After the Ecstasy, the Laundry*, that
I have never forgotten:

> The Understanding of emptiness [genuine openness, accept-
> ance, and freedom] is contagious. It appears we can catch it
> from one another. We know that when a sad or angry person
> enters a room, we too often enter that sadness or anger. It
> shouldn't surprise us then, that the presence of a teacher who
> is empty, open, awake can have a powerful effect on another
> person, especially if that person is ripe.

Even the words written by sages of ordinariness can impact
us—*if* we let them.

THE WORDS AND THEMES
OF WISDOM FIGURES

Rabbi Abraham Heschel, in his work *God in Search of Man*, once pointed out that he felt that people seemed attuned to their environment long before they truly became aware of who they were. He then added to this point: "Many of us are [also] conscious of the hiddenness of things, but few of us sense the mystery of our own presence." What he is implying here is that we are called to be open, honest, and self-confident enough to spend less energy on defense and a lack of appreciation of self and more on a discovery of who we are—simply, and unvarnished, *ordinary*.

As we have just seen with respect to mentors that the impact of someone like Heschel who is able to fill a mentoring or teaching role can be the essential element in our prizing of ordinariness. Pat Schneider, in *Writing Alone and with Others*, notes, "I tried to avoid teachers who would want me to sound like them. I wanted to sound like myself. Finding the teacher or mentor who is right for you is worth the search. Shop around, and above all, trust your own instincts." She then lists aspects of what she believes "a good teacher" is and does. Although she is speaking about writing I think the same can be said about discovering one's ordinary self:

I. A good teacher assists you to sound more and more like your own self and less and less like the teacher.

2. A good teacher always tells you the strengths of your writing, as well as the weaknesses. If your teacher cannot identify the strength in your writing voice, then he or she has no right to address what is mitigating against that strength. Do not subject yourself to a teacher who only gives negative feedback.

3. A good teacher knows more than you do, is willing to give to you what he or she knows, and rejoices when you find your own way of using what you have been given.

4. A good teacher believes in you and lets you know it.

5. A good teacher gives you an honest (perhaps sometimes hard to hear) response, but always acknowledges that all responses are subjective.

6. A good teacher encourages you to listen to other opinions and take only those critical suggestions that strengthen and encourage your voice.

7. A good teacher does not inhabit a pedestal.

8. A good teacher admits that he or she has sometimes been mistaken, wrongheaded, or unhelpful.

9. A good teacher engages you with affection and keeps appropriate boundaries.

10. A good teacher lets you go when the time to go has come.

Being "a good teacher" of ordinariness also requires the deep belief that imitating others' good traits may be wonderful. Whereas, seeking to impersonate them—no matter how great the person may be—is to forfeit your own self. This is not easy for some mentors. The father of writer Alexandra Fuller knew this well. In her book, *Leaving Before the Rains Come*, she reports him saying to her at one point, "'Letting other people row their own boats,' Dad said. 'That's the tricky bit.'"

The danger of forfeiting our own sense of ordinariness and some mentors not fathoming the importance of calling people to be all that they can be without asking them to become someone else, no matter how good that person may be, is a palpable danger in seeking and offering guidance. Thomas Merton once wrote,

> Many poets are not poets for the same reason that many religious men are not saints: they never succeed in being themselves. . . . They wear out their minds and bodies in a hopeless endeavor to have somebody else's experiences or . . . possess somebody else's sanctity. . . . They waste their years. . . . For many absurd reasons they are convinced that they are obliged to become somebody else who died two hundred years ago and lived in circumstances utterly alien to their own.

Shunryu Suzuki echoed this theme during a formal private interview with a student. When the student repeated something Suzuki had previously said in a lecture, the Zen master shook his head that this was wrong.

The student was obviously taken off-guard and indicated that it was what he Master had actually said himself. To this, Suzuki responded: "When I said it, it was true. When you said it, it was false." Mimicking others—even those who are deserving of our respect and whose teachings are worthy of our examination—will not enhance our ordinary selves.

Portals to ordinariness are opened in different, creative ways by persons who truly see the value of "simply" being yourself. This may be demonstrated as a tenet of avoiding the pitfalls of egoism, as a way of offering space to others to have the freedom to be themselves rather than, as was just mentioned, mimic others, or as part of an artistic pursuit of ordinariness, such as writing one's own memoir.

Mary Karr, in her work *The Art of Memoir*, addresses the importance of authenticity in the author's own voice in sharing biographical material. This is worth noting, since it is akin to the sharing of our authentic and ordinary selves in many ways.

Recently, a friend I teach with talked me down off the ledge about [writing *The Art of Memoir*] by reminding me that I've spent decades talking with joy to students about memoir. What I really bring to the classroom is having cherished the form as long and as hard as anybody. In 1965 I wrote, "When I grow up, I will write ½ poetry and ½ autobiography." And as a strange child reading the sagas of Helen Keller and Maya Angelou, I just felt less lonely. In some animistic way, I believed they were talking (as my toddler son once said of the infuriatingly saccharine Mr. Rogers) "only to me."

In providing greater detail as to the importance of not exaggerating, minimizing, or lying to yourself in understanding and sharing your story, she added later in her book:

> Trying to help students diagnose their own blind spots, I often ask the following questions:
>
> 1. What do people usually like and dislike about you? You should reflect both aspects in your pages.
>
> 2. How do you want to be perceived, and in what ways have you ever been false or posed as other than who you are? (Lovers/family members yelling at you when they're mad have answered this one for you, btw.)
>
> 3. Is there any verbal signpost you can look for that suggests you're posturing? One kid I know started bringing in references to metal bands to show how cool he was. I might start yakking about philosophy.

Annie Dillard also uses the metaphor of writing in general, as opposed to preparing a memoir, to point to the need to be open to "revisions" in viewing ourselves that also applies to unearthing more of our ordinary selves rather than to hold onto what is habitual or somehow learned. She writes, "Several delusions weaken the writer's resolve to throw away work. If he has read his pages too often, those pages will have a necessary quality, the ring of the inevitable, like poetry known by heart; they will perfectly answer their own familiar rhythms."

Dillard also sees not simply habit but effort spent on learning something as a block to unlearning so there is space for new information. To make her point she writes,

> A cabdriver sang his songs to me, in New York. Some we sang together. He had turned the meter off; he drove around midtown, singing. One long song he sang twice; it was the only dull one. I said, "You already sang that one; let's sing something else." And he said, "You don't know how long it took me to get that one together."

From other angles, Zen master Shunryu Suzuki also addresses the value of "just being yourself." In a book containing some of his teaching sessions (*Not Always So*) he attends to the values of clarity, sincerity, humility, and the dynamics of ordinariness. His teachings encourage a constant sense of awareness of the one constant in life: *change*. To him, honoring the truth of ordinariness "means to be yourself, always yourself, without sticking to an old self."

In this regard, his teachings include the two following, simple but pointed statements:

> The important thing it to be able to enjoy your life without being fooled by things.
>
> When you are fooled by something else, the damage won't be so big. But when you are fooled by yourself, it is fatal. No more medicine.

To accomplish such a sense of sincerity and openness, he shares that

> when I know what I am doing clearly, without any overes-timation or underestimation, very honestly and truly, I do not have much burden on my mind. Zazen [sitting medi-tation] practice especially has been a great help. If I hadn't been practicing zazen, I wouldn't have survived in the way I did. I started my practice when I was quite young. But even more, I started my practice in its true sense [as an adult] after I came to San Francisco.

Later he adds the following point about meditation that is di-rectly related to enhancing the spirit of ordinariness: "We do not practice zen to attain special enlightenment. Just to be our-selves and just to be free from our useless efforts or tendencies, we practice zazen."

Interestingly, his own process of self-awareness involved not the *correction* of all of his growing edges (those areas that seem to need improvement) but the focusing on improvement as a way of reaping an indirect bounty of the process: *humility*. He felt that when we work on our character it helps us become free of our ego in ways not probable if we hadn't made efforts that may still not lead to the direct successes we wish.

In line with the recognition of the almost impossible na-ture of completely altering certain character traits, he asked his followers not to have demands of others to change as we would want them to at a pace we would expect and "thereby break their good hearts." His desire to combine gentleness, ordinariness, and pacing was evident and worthy of emulation in the way we treat ourselves and others. I still remember pacing a colleague too fast and him finally resisting with the comment, "This is how I am. I can't change that." I had good goals and ones he probably could have gotten closer to, but I did not honor the difficulty for him to reach them in ways that would not do harm to how he could more completely open up his total self.

One of the other areas Shunryu Suzuki emphasized that is so compelling in his writing is his emphasis on the "soil" (our attitude) in which authenticity, and thus ordinariness, can grow and blossom. Again, in his words:

> Most of us study Buddhism as though it were something that was already given to us. We think that what we should do is preserve the Buddha's teaching, like putting food in the refrigerator. Then to study Buddhism we take the food out of the refrigerator. Whenever you want it, it is already there. Instead, Zen students should be interested in how to produce food from the field, from the garden. We put the emphasis on the ground.

In the search for understanding our ordinary selves and to live with peace and joy, we can take his statement and replace the word "Buddhism" with the word "life" and change the reference to Zen students to students of life. What he says here applies to anyone searching for a larger way to understand themselves and live life.

From still another vantage point, Brother David Steindl-Rast, in his book *Gratefulness, the Heart of Prayer*, which is to my mind a contemporary classic in Western Christianity, writes about the self in ways that would also resonate with persons from the East. In his case, his contribution to the topic of ordinariness emphasizes compassion that is ego-less:

It is the concept of self that expands when we come to understand what love really means. The current idea of love identifies our self with our little individualistic ego. This little ego translates "Love thy neighbor as thyself" into a series of incredible mental acrobatics. Step one: imagine you are someone else. Step two: try to whip up a passionate attraction for that imaginary other. Step three: try to feel for someone who is really someone else the same passionate attraction you felt for yourself (if you did) when you were imagining that you were someone else. That's asking a little much, isn't it? And yet, the command is so simple: "Love your neighbor as (being) yourself." That means: realize that your self is not limited to your little ego. Your true self includes your neighbor. You belong together—radically so. If you know what self means, you know what belonging means. It costs you no effort to belong to yourself. Spontaneously, you say "yes" to yourself in your heart. But at heart you are one with all others. Your heart knows that your true self includes your neighbor. Love means that you say "yes" from your heart to that true self—and act on it accordingly.

Steindl-Rast has no illusion as to how hard being a loving, grateful person can be in contemporary society. Yet, when persons no longer see themselves as needy and are less ego driven, their relationships thrive as well. Meaning replaces success, generativity stands in place of grasping, and we begin to see not only ourselves but the world differently. As our values change, so does our life.

We can see this from yet another vantage point in the writings of Rabbi Abraham Joshua Heschel. The poetic and philosophical flavor of his words break through the utilitarian sense of contemporary life. They call us to search for and embrace a sense of our "extra-ordinary" self and roles. In *Questions Man Asks*, he writes: "It is not enough for me to be able to say 'I am'; I want to know *who I am*, and in relation to whom I live. It is not enough for me to ask questions; I want to know how to answer the one question that seems to encompass everything I face: What am I here for?" Later he adds that a person "must time and again decide which direction to take. The course of his life is, accordingly, unpredictable; no one can write his autobiography in advance."

In line with this, he unveils the trap of induced neediness and entitlement. Instead of enabling us to embrace justice and understand the inheritance of being a human being, it detours us. In *Man Is Not Alone* among the points he notes is:

> We usually fail to discern between authentic needs and, misjudging a whim for an aspiration, we are thrown into

ugly tensions. Most obsessions are the perpetuation of such misjudgments. In fact, more people die in epidemics of needs than in epidemics of disease.

These words are not only for us but also for those who follow us. Valuing and living out of the ordinary self requires awareness and respect. As Heschel notes in another of his works, *The Insecurity of Freedom*:

> We prepare the pupil for employment, for holding a job. We do not teach him how to be a person, how to resist conformity, how to grow inwardly, how to say no to his own self. We teach him how to adjust to the public; we do not teach him how to cultivate privacy.

He adds later,

> We tell the pupil many things, but what has our instruction to do with his inner problems, with the way he is going to behave or think outside of the classroom? In our classrooms we shy away from fundamental issues. How should one deal with evil? What shall one do about evil? What is the meaning of honesty? How should one face the problem of loneliness?

Finally, in line with these questions and in keeping with the theme of ordinariness, in his book *God in Search of Man*, he states:

> We teach children how to measure, how to weigh. We fail to teach them how to revere, how to sense wonder and awe.

The words and sense of presence of true mentors in ordinariness are not limited, of course, to what has been sampled here. Overall, though, the attitude we seek in receiving and offering such mentoring in the spirit of self-discovery of the ordinary self requires at its basis an attitude that negates the ego to become a clearer vessel for discovery, not the imposition of a personal will outside ourselves. Sometimes a mentor may wish to tell someone what they would prefer. Instead, there needs to be an openness to possibility that lies even beyond what we believe are our positive wishes.

Elie Wiesel describes such an encounter at its ideal with respect to his contacts with Rebbe Menachem Schneerson, arguably one of the most influential rabbis in modern history, in sharing:

> I Know of no one who left the Rebbe without being deeply affected if not changed by the encounter. . . . Time in his presence begins running at a different pace. . . . In his presence, you come closer in touch with your inner center of gravity. Whenever I would see the Rebbe, he touched the depths in me. That was true of everyone who came to see the Rebbe. Somehow, when the person left, he or she felt that they had lived deeper and . . . on a higher level.

When the Rebbe himself was asked, "What's a Rebbe good for?" he didn't respond with a feeling of having been insulted or being shown disrespect. Instead he replied,

I can't speak for myself, but I can tell you about my own Rebbe [his father-in-law]. For me, my Rebbe was the geologist of the soul. You see, there are so many treasures in the earth. There is gold, there is silver, and there are diamonds. But if you don't know where to dig, you'll only find dirt and rocks and mud. The Rebbe can tell you where to dig, and what to dig for, but the digging you must do for yourself.[3]

Sometimes such encounters are with "mentors of the moment" who, in the world's eyes, may be seen of little worth themselves. This is what Jean Vanier, philosopher, theologian, humanitarian, and founder of *L'Arche*, a worldwide federation that concerns itself with persons with intellectual disabilities, found to be true. He reported that in 1964, when he visited an asylum for men with mental handicaps, he found it to be "a horrific place, full of screaming and violence; and yet it filled me with a sense of wonderment. I sensed in these men a great cry—'Do you love me?' 'Will you come back?'" He then decided to visit other similar settings that he found equally distressing and decided to act. These persons with disabilities were his mentors in the discernment of how he would live out his life. Because of his openness to the voice of possibility that was very much in line with who he was in his own ordinariness and simplicity, an international movement for good began.

May we have the good fortune to meet someone like that. Even of possibly greater import: may we be our ordinary selves at times to the extent that people will be able to feel and be more totally themselves for having been with us so they know where to search inside to find "the diamonds of ordinariness."

SIX

ALONETIME: EMBRACING SPACES CONDUCIVE TO THE PROCESS OF SELF-UNCOVERING AND RE-DISCOVERING

Solitude is the furnace in which transformation takes place.
—HENRI J. M. NOUWEN, *Way of the Heart*

Solitude is a stern mother who brooks no nonsense. And the question arises—am I so full of nonsense that she will cast me out? I pray that she will not.
—THOMAS MERTON, *A Vow of Conversation*

The Sabbath [is] an opportunity to mend our tattered lives; to collect rather than dissipate time.
—ABRAHAM JOSHUA HESCHEL, *The Sabbath*

Early in my professional career, an unexpected occurrence included an unforeseen invitation that has, to this day, changed life for me. The publication of one of my books encouraged the director of a graduate program at St. Michael's College in Vermont to inquire whether I would be willing to teach a three-week summer course. Given the beautiful setting

near Lake Champlain I thought it would be a great opportunity
to enjoy the local scenery and get things done, since the teaching
load was light and they were providing a townhouse for my use.

My expectations were more than met with respect to the
natural beauty of the setting. Rudyard Kipling reportedly said
that the two settings for the finest sunsets on a lake were Lake
Victoria in Africa and Lake Champlain from the Vermont side.
Also, the lush mountains, chance for scenic ferry rides, and
beautiful walking trails up Mt. Mansfield made relaxing walks
a special pleasure. The space in which to write and prepare
lectures for a new faculty position I was beginning in the fall
also proved to be available, as did a chance to interact with wonderful faculty and students. However, the hidden jewel in all of
this that proved to be a total surprise was something less tan-
gible but more life changing: *extended periods of silence and solitude.*

Initially, I had responded to them with an urge for activity
or an experience of discomfort. How would I "productively"
fill the space was the initial question for me. Yet, recalling a discussion I had had with fellow psychologist and spiritual writer
Henri Nouwen a few years earlier while sitting in his kitchen
in his little apartment off Harvard Square I finally recognized
something new for me: I needed more space to "simply be."

During that meeting with Henri, I was enthusiastic about
the need to be available to others, especially since my work as
a therapist, clinical supervisor, mentor, and presenter even back
then was primarily with professional helpers and healers in the

fields of medicine, nursing, psychology, social work, counseling, education, and ministry. He responded with encouragement and appreciation of my efforts. However, he was also adamant that "availability is not simply a gift for many of us. It is a problem."

Since he was also a priest, I was not surprised when he then said that there must be a theme from sacred scripture that responds to this issue. When I asked him what he thought it might be, he said that nothing came immediately to mind, so we simply let it drop. Finally, just before I was to leave for the airport to fly back home, his face lit up and he said, *"Pruning! That's it.* That is the theme from the bible that I was trying to recall. When you prune something, it doesn't blossom less, it flowers more deeply." He then spoke to me about a way to begin a more profound appreciation of this. From it would naturally arise an appreciation of pruning, where it would be needed and, as I would learn later, on my own, the pain involved in the required trimming of psychological branches (activities, thoughts, and beliefs) that had driven me to the point of burnout on several occasions.

His advice did not turn out to be a long dissertation or details from a philosophy of living he wished me to adopt. Instead, it involved a simple, gentle nudge to take some time out in silence and solitude each morning and let it lead me where it would. What he shared was very much in line with the questions posed in his book *The Genesee Diary*: "Is there a quiet stream underneath the fluctuating affirmations and rejections of my little world? Is there a still point where my life is anchored and from which I can reach out with hope and courage and confidence?"

He would also add the following in a foreword to another book, a description of reality that bespeaks the need for silence and, at times, solitude:

> Our lives are fragmented. There are so many things to do, so many events to worry about, so many people to think of, so many experiences to work through, so many tasks to fulfill, so many demands to respond to, and so many needs to pay attention to. Often it seems that just keeping things together asks for enormous energy. Different powers pull us into different directions and our sense of unity and togetherness is constantly threatened. This fragmentation is probably one of the most painful experiences of modern men and women. . . . Underneath the running and rushing of modern life often lurks the nagging feeling of being disconnected, alienated and bored. Although we are busy we experience ourselves as the passive victims of great powers that control us and seem very hard to resist.[1]

Nowhere do I feel this is more evident than when we take the time to quiet ourselves, reflect, breathe deeply, and simply seek to enjoy our ordinary selves. For, although I followed Nouwen's suggestions prior to my times teaching in Vermont, the longer periods of experiencing such alonetime that began at St. Michael's would prove crucial in my life and psychological travels with other helpers and healers who turned to me for guidance in their own lives and clinical practices.

As I created open spaces in my schedule and consciousness, those thoughts, feelings, beliefs, and suppressed experiences, attitudes, and emotions lying just beyond the surface of my awareness now rose to the surface. In allowing them to flow without censure, interference, or an undue need to entertain, attend to, avoid, or fix them, they turned out to be inner mentors of ordinariness. When I was nonjudgmental but simply observant of them they taught me ways in which I had created an identity, needs, and a style of living and responding that were alien to my ordinary self. To some extent, these experiences were like one expressed by Sara Maitland in her volume *A Book of Silence*, when she shares, "I felt oddly foxy—I'd slipped my leash and got away. I felt open to whatever might happen and hungry for the silence." She added what was also true in my case: "It took a little while to realize how much I loved it. It was not a sudden plunge into solitude and silence; it was a gradual shifting of gears, a gentle movement toward a new way of living that gave me an increasing deep satisfaction." In my own experience at that time and since then, I felt and feel to this day the words of Ezra Pound: "I did not enter silence. Silence entered me."

Noted explorer Erling Kagge, who is the first person to have completed the Three Poles Challenge on foot—the North Pole, the South Pole, and the summit of Mount Everest—also reinforced my thinking, in his book *Silence*, with the following reflections:

I no longer try to create absolute silence around me. The silence that I am after is the silence within.

. . . .

In a way, silence is . . . about getting inside what you are doing. Experiencing rather than overthinking. Allowing each moment to be big enough.

. . . .

Life is long, if we listen to ourselves often enough, and look up.

. . . .

You cannot wait first to get quiet. Not in New York, nor anywhere else. You must create your own silence.

Kagge also notes in his book about silence in an age of noise:

Wonder is the very engine of life. But my children are thirteen, sixteen and nineteen years old and wonder less and less; if they still wonder at anything, they quickly pull out their smartphones to find the answer. They are still curious, but their faces are not as childish, more adult, and their heads are now filled with more ambitions than questions.

However, our ordinary self, who people get a glimpse of in public, depends to a great degree on what we experience in that space called "alonetime." Alonetime, as discussed earlier, can be described as a period of silence and solitude or even those times when we are simply being quietly reflective when in a group setting. For instance, I have found that many insights have spontaneously arrived when I was quiet during a flight, on a drive, or on a train, even when others were present.

With respect to finding your own ordinary self, in existentialist psychologist Jouard's book *The Transparent Self*, he takes a view similar to what I have been sharing about my own inner journey:

> Freedom from the experienced impact of others' physical or psychological presence is the first step in the fulfillment of freedom-to-grow. Artists, writers, scientists and performers who aim at endless actualization of their possibilities attest to the need for solitude. They need it for meditation, rehearsal, and undisturbed pursuit of their ideas. One usually needs to leave other people in order to take leave of the way one has chronically been with them. This being-with embodies both a pledge from the one person to appear before the others as he has in the past (the ways with which they are familiar and with which they can cope without strain to themselves), and pressure from the others to remain as he has been. "Going away" can be, and usually is, the first step in psychological growth. One need not be in solitude to redefine, or to discover a new being-for-oneself. One can go to a new place, where one's roles have not as yet been congealed in the minds of others. Privacy can be found among crowds of strangers. The problem faced by a person who has less mobility is how to change the concept that others have of him into a new one which encompasses his new phases of growth. Other

people—close relatives and friends especially—tend to invalidate new ways of being that are disclosed by someone whom they have long known.

The impact of such times can be amazing. In his biography of Zen master Shunryu Suzuki, the author, David Chadwick, provides the following brief vignette to illustrate just one example of how such moments and movements to be with a different support group can profoundly free us to be our ordinary selves again or maybe for the first time:

> A Stanford professor told Suzuki that many college students were smoking marijuana all the time and taking LSD. Maybe it was good in some ways for them to experiment, but it was interfering with their studies. What did Suzuki [who led a local Zen center] do about this problem? "Oh, nothing," said Suzuki. "I just teach them how to sit zazen [quiet meditation], and they forget about those things pretty soon."

For Suzuki, "Life without [sitting meditation] is like winding our clock without setting it. It runs perfectly well but doesn't tell time."

Often such a journey to experience greater inner peace and to better understand our ordinary selves begins with a desire or fantasy. Sandy Johnson, in her book *The Book of Tibetan Elders*, describes this wish quite well when she writes,

> Fascinated, I read about a people who believe in the existence of a mystical kingdom of Shambala, a beautiful city where

extraordinary beings live, cut off from the outside world by their own volition. It is a place of peace; its only weapons are bows and arrows that have the nature of exalted wisdom and are more powerful than all the destructive missiles in the outside world. Some Tibetans view Shambala as metaphor for one's own inner spiritual journey and dedicate their lives to finding it within themselves.

Yet, the attentive quiet of meditation, which is an intense sense of alonetime, is more than a fantasy or an act of self-centeredness. It is an education in wise living. As Matthieu Ricard notes in his book *Happiness*,

Indeed, meditation is not about sitting quietly in the shade of a tree and relaxing in a moment of respite from the daily grind; it is about familiarizing yourself with a new vision of things, a new way to manage your thoughts, of perceiving people and experiencing the world.

To this he adds:

We willingly spend a dozen years in school, then go on to college or professional training for several more; we work out at the gym to stay healthy; we spend a lot of time enhancing our comfort, our wealth, and our social status. We put a great deal into all this, and yet we do so little to improve the inner condition that determines the very quality of our lives. What strange hesitancy, fear, or apathy stops us from looking within ourselves, from trying to grasp the true essence of joy and sadness, desire and hatred? Fear of the unknown prevails, and the courage to explore that inner world fails at the frontier of our mind.

From a seemingly different position are the views of Clark Strand, as presented in his eminently readable and helpful book on meditation, *The Wooden Bowl*. In an effort not to discourage those who would wish to spend several minutes or longer by slowing down, being attentively quiet, and experiencing the present moment in a fresh, open manner, his main guideline is "to maintain a light spirit of friendliness with regard to what you are doing" by sitting quietly with no expectations. He adds, "It's nothing special but it works."

In his own words, he shares that taking time to sit or walk in silence is like a hobby:

> [It] ought to be a time when you can occupy your mind with something for its own sake, without getting caught up in any of your usual preoccupations: Am I doing this right? Are the others doing it better? . . . It ought to be an area of your life where you can let go of the obsessive desire to improve yourself, to get ahead, or to do better than anybody else. . . . [It] ought to decrease the drivenness of our lives, not make it worse. . . . The person who meditates—whether for five minutes or five hours a day—wants to keep one area of his or her life that is not driven, that does not draw them ceaselessly away from the fundamental *enoughness, sanity,* and *beauty* of the world.

And, I would add, *ourselves*.

In his book *Wisdom of the Desert*, Thomas Merton connected the themes of meditation and ordinariness in his work on the fourth- and fifth-century Desert Fathers (*Abbas*) and Mothers (*Ammas*) (discussed in Chapter I). He wrote:

> These monks insisted on remaining human and "ordinary." This may seem to be a paradox, but it is very important. If we reflect for a moment, we will see that to fly into the desert in order to be extraordinary is only to carry the world with you as an implicit standard of comparison. The result would be nothing but self-contemplation and self-comparison with the negative standard of the world one had abandoned. Some of the monks of the desert did this, as a matter of fact, and the only fruit of their troubles was that they went out of their heads. The simple men who lived their lives out to a good old age among the rocks and sands only did so because they had come into the desert to be themselves, their ordinary selves.

To appreciate this more deeply sometimes requires places where we can feel the space to relish alonetime. It may also require guidance from those who know how to embrace both ordinariness and alonetime. Buddhist psychologist and meditation teacher Jack Kornfield notes that you would not want to go hiking in the Himalayas without a guide, so why would you want to travel the even more demanding trails of the inner life without the guidance that is available?

PLACES AND PEOPLE
OF ALONETIME

In Peter France's book, *Patmos: A Place of Healing*, he describes how this island held an aura of possibility for him, noting that "the island of Patmos is a place of power. It changes people. They come here for a brief summer visit and find themselves returning, year after year, for the rest of their lives. If you ask them why, they all give the same answer: they are responding to a force which they can recognize but not explain. And which they find nowhere else."

There are, of course, other dramatic stories of "places" and "people" of solitude worth noting. In them, the authors' comments demonstrate how being alone in a quiet space helped them find their ordinary selves, rather than remain being caught in a societal or personally destructive cycle. One such story is by Erwin James, who wrote in *The Guardian* (30 September 2004) a brief reflection on the time he spent in prison:

> I have never minded having those 20 years taken from me. . . .
> If I had not had them taken away, they would most likely have
> been wasted anyway. . . . My cell then was a reinforced concrete
> box and I spent the biggest part of my days locked behind
> its steel door. I spent a lot of time reading and meditating
> on what I had read, until the fear and anxiety I had felt from
> being held in those conditions gradually subsided. . . . I could

not say exactly when it happened—and I am not sure that I realized it until sometime afterwards—but there was definitely a period in that cell when for the first time in my life I experienced peace. I had not expected to miss any aspects of my imprisonment when I had been released. But more than once during these past few weeks of being out and about full-time in the modern world, I have missed that.

Another example of extreme solitude is given by Christine Ritter, in her book *Woman in the Polar Night*. She wrote the following about her extended stay in Svalbard, Norway, which demonstrates how one can experience the self so intensely in silence and solitude: "How varied are the experiences one lives through in the Artic. One can murder and devour, calculate and measure, one can go out of one's mind from loneliness and terror, and one can certainly also go mad with enthusiasm for the all-too-overwhelming beauty. But it is also true that one will never experience in the Artic anything that one has not one-self brought there." She adds later in her book, "in centuries to come, men will go to the Artic as in biblical times they withdrew to the desert, to find the truth again." In his introduction to her book, Lawrence Millman writes: "I can't imagine any [other] polar explorer making a statement like this."

Polar explorer Admiral William Byrd wrote in his book, *Alone*, a sentiment similar to Ritter's and James': [I had] one man's desire to know that kind of experience [of solitude] to the full, to be by himself for a while and to taste peace and quiet

and solitude long enough to find out how good they really are."
He also said, "Now, I wanted something more than just privacy in the geographical sense. I wanted to sink roots into some
replenishing philosophy."

After his ordeal alone, he wrote several years after his experience: "I did take away something that I had not fully possessed
before: appreciation of the sheer beauty and miracle of being
alive, and a humble set of values.... Civilization has not altered
my ideas. I live more simply now, and with more peace." Truly,
this sounds like a fruit of embracing the virtue of ordinariness.

The capacity to be alone certainly is also seen today as an
aspect of emotional maturity. British psychiatrist Edwin Storr
suggests no less in his book *Solitude: A Return to the Self*. Relying on
the psychoanalytic thinker Donald Winnicott, who was one of
the first modern psychological thinkers to discuss the positive
aspects of solitude, he notes the connection between the capacity to be alone and such essential processes as self-discovery
and self-realization. He goes on to say that meditation (or silent
prayer for religious persons), for example, can

> facilitate integration by allowing time for previously unre-
> lated thoughts and feelings to interact. Being able to get in
> touch with one's deepest thoughts and feelings, and providing
> time for them to regroup themselves into new formations and
> combinations, are important aspects of the creative process,
> as well as a way of relieving tension and promoting mental
> health. It appears, therefore, that some development of the

capacity to be alone is necessary if the brain is to function at its best and if the individual is to fulfil his highest potential. Human beings easily become alienated from their own deepest needs and feelings. Learning, thinking, innovation, and maintaining contact with one's inner world are all facilitated by solitude.

It is not surprising, then, that an understanding of one's true ordinariness depends so heavily on the need to take time to be in silence and solitude and to open oneself up in ways not possible when constantly being stimulated or unreflective during group activity.

Is it any wonder that American novelist, memoirist, biographer, literary critic, and essayist Doris Grumbach, in her book *Fifty Days of Solitude*, reports, after experiencing a significant period of solitude, that what I term "our ordinary self" as a way of living out one's life becomes more possible. She writes:

> There was a reward for this deprivation. The absence of other voices compelled me to listen more intently to the inner one. I became aware that the interior voice, so often before stifled or stilled by what I thought others wanted to hear, or what I considered to be socially acceptable, grew gratifyingly louder, more insistent.

However, she is also aware of our natural resistance to such periods of detachment from society when she adds:

How right Rousseau was about the modern person. Our points of reference are always our neighbors, the people in the village or our city, our acquaintances at school, at games, at work, our close and distant families, all of whom tell us, with their hundreds of tongues, who we are. . . . Rarely if ever did we think to look within for knowledge of ourselves. Were we afraid? Perhaps, we thought we would find nothing there."

Solitude and silence share with the virtue of ordinariness the need for courage in face of such fears and others like them. In this sense, it is a virtue that truly is for the self-aware, sane, person who possesses inner freedom.

Jack Kornfield, in his book *The Wise Heart*, sees meditation as the space to face the questions of life, our own questions. In his own reflection about this form of mindfulness practice and Buddhist psychology, he raises the questions:

Was it a need to take a deep breath and find a wiser way to cope with conflict, stress, and fears so common in modern life? Was it the longing for a psychology that included the spiritual dimension and the highest human potential in its vision of healing? Was it a hope to find simple ways to quiet the mind and open the heart?

Thomas Merton, a monk and author of a number of books, including his bestselling autobiographical work, *Seven Story Mountain*, lived in community for much of his religious life. However, at a certain point he was given permission to live in a hermitage. The joy of his reaction is one that echoes those of others who had such opportunities through the ages. In his own words:

> What a thing it is to sit absolutely alone in the forest at night, cherished by this wonderful, unintelligible, perfectly innocent speech . . . the talk that rain makes all by itself all over the ridges. . . . As long as it talks I am going to listen. But I am going to sleep, because here in this wilderness I have learned to sleep again.

Such periods need not be the result of physical separation. It can be at moments when quiet prevails. Possibly it is in the early morning before the rest of the house awakens, an evening bath after everyone is asleep, or a mother's moments during a night feeding of her baby. Periods like this can be renewing, refreshing, and enlightening because the "dust of the day" has settled and we can hear the thoughts from within that have been shut out by the din of the day. It is at such times that prolonged periods of silence may have greater import in terms of the broader sense of our ordinary selves—our personal narrative. Maitland recognized this during some time apart early in her experiments with time spent in silence and solitude.

> One of the things I gained during this week, in this specific silence, was a much stronger narrative of my own life. It was not until after I went home that I became aware of how

much—how many anecdotes—I had added to my conscious memory bank. The effort to eliminate ego and silence the mind, heart and imagination destroys a clear sense of time and therefore of narrative, but the attempt to use silence deliberately to stimulate internal states of imagination has exactly the opposite effect. . . . You go out into the wild and you "discover who you are," "establish your individual voice," or "your authentic identity." One of the definitions of identity or selfhood being explored at present in both philosophy and psychiatry is the idea that the ability to construct a coherent narrative of one's own life circumscribes identity—to be an individual is to own a narrative of self. Choosing to be alone, solitary, particularly in a place that is "sublime," is one way of establishing contact with such a narrative, unmediated by other people's interpretation.

Andrew Weiss, in his book *Beginning Mindfulness*, echoes this with respect to placing ourselves in the now with our eyes wide open. He comments:

Meditation is not just something you do on a cushion or chair. Anything you do is an occasion to engage yourself mindfully in the present moment. . . . Ultimately the path of mindfulness will lead you to a place within yourself where you may encounter the world without ideas or preconceptions, where you can disengage from your habitual narrative and free yourself from mental constructs [which], . . . gives us a way through suffering to joy.

Beyond the freeing effects described by Maitland and Weiss, there are many specific benefits of alonetime when we consider discovering and embracing our ordinary selves. When we have periods of silence and possibly solitude or pay attention to what is going on around and within us without immediately judging, stopping, or pondering our observations, we can experience such gifts as:

- Opportunities to relax, lean back from roles, and be able to be in the moment
- Being able to take walks where we are experiencing what is around us rather than being in a cognitive envelope
- Experiencing an attitude of simplicity by being present to where we are, not where we want to be or running from where we have been
- Enjoying our relationship with ourselves more and needing the reinforcement of others less
- Seeing the thoughts and sense of anger, entitlement, grasping, cowardice, and fear that may be lying just below the surface and acting as invisible puppeteers during the day
- Recognizing and embracing the natural changes that will always occur in one's life
- Observing the unknotting of complexities into manageable challenges that seem to get less burdensome or overwhelming in the process
- Becoming more intrigued about who we really are, what narrative we have been sold, and what sense of ordinary self can be explored further, and further

- A desire to unlearn and see things differently than others have claimed and that we may in turn have embraced as part of enculturation
- More freedom to observe and receive life's smaller things as true gifts instead of submitting to the environment's advertisement that more is better
- Less of a desire to compare oneself with others but instead seek to trace the paths of one's own development
- A greater ability to laugh at oneself
- Surprising insights that lift us out of habitual thought patterns
- Increasing freedom from the anxieties and preoccupations that tend to represent the "white noise" of much of the day
- Increasing in our mind the value of leaning back from the constant activities and emotions of the normal routine
- Forgoing the comfort of denial for the true peace of having the courage to face and embrace what we must in life
- Recognizing new spaces in our life (in the shower, between phone calls, short walk at lunch, just before we fall asleep or get out of bed, on the drive home) to take a breath instead of simply rushing to our grave and calling that practical
- Protecting our inner fire so when the time calls for it we can reach out without being pulled down
- A deeper appreciation for transparency, authenticity, simplicity, humility, and honesty as fruits of true ordinariness

Beyond this, in simple terms, Jack Kornfield recognizes that mindful periods "allow us the space of kindness. There is beauty in the ordinary. We invite the heart to sit on the front porch and experience from a place of rest the inevitable comings and goings of emotions and events, the struggles and successes of the world."

In an interview, writer Anne LaMotte echoes this sentiment in a response to the question, "In your book, *Bird by Bird*, I was taken by author Geneen Roth's insight that awareness is learning to keep yourself company. Can you say more?" She responds:

> The idea, especially for women and girls, is that you're sup-posed to become great company. In the 50s and 60s, when all the power was in the hands of men, you wanted men to find you brilliant and entertaining. But doing that you lose con-nection with your own crazy, beautiful, mixed-up, obtuse self. Becoming friends with *that* person and looking in the mirror and saying "Hi" is the beginning of new life. It's not being full of yourself in the pejorative sense. It's like, "Wow, I'm full of myself, my little self, my higher self, and all the selves I've ever been."[2]

I would simply add to this more specifically, being full of and appreciating the beauty of the *ordinary* self. Rediscovering the lost virtue of ordinariness certainly is enhanced by our seeking and embracing periods of alonetime. As in the case of the other points made in this book, one of its special gifts is that it allows us to return home to ourselves—*again.*

Epilogue: Returning Home to Yourself . . . *Again*

The thing that is really hard, and really amazing, is giving up on being perfect and beginning the work of becoming yourself.
—Anna Quindlen

Live as if you were living a second time, and as though you had acted wrongly the first time.
—Viktor Frankl, *Man's Search for Inner Meaning*

A reporter interviewing a 104-year-old woman asked, "And what do you think is the best thing about being 104?" She replied, "No peer pressure."
—Terry Hershey, *The Power of Pause*

We can certainly exist, maybe occasionally live, without appreciating our ordinary selves and others for who they really are in relaxed moments of their own full self-acceptance of both their gifts and growing edges. Rarely does someone die from *not* appreciating their own sense of ordinariness. The question under such circumstances, though, is whether we really live—and live in a way that also sets the stage so other people's lives may be enhanced by our welcoming presence. To truly fathom our ordinariness is not easy. It takes the courage to understand our total self as a way of *embracing the generative legacy of our family and culture on the one hand, and knowing what needs to be left behind, on the other.* This takes consideration on our part of what might truly comprise our "ordinary self" in its fullness rather than letting it solely be defined by what or how others might wish us to be—or not be!

David Brooks, once again in his book *Road to Character*, sets the challenge before us quite well in terms of what it means to live an un-reflected life with respect to our sense of self within:

> Years pass and the deepest parts of yourself go unexplored and unstructured. You are busy, but you have a vague anxiety that your life has not achieved its ultimate meaning and sig- nificance. You live with an unconscious boredom, not really loving, not really attached to the moral purposes that give life its worth. You lack the internal criteria to make unshakable commitments. You never develop inner constancy, the integ- rity that can withstand popular disapproval or a serious blow. You find yourself doing things that other people approve of, whether these things are right for you or not. You foolishly judge other people by their abilities, not by their worth. You do not have a strategy to build character, and without that, not only your inner life but also your external life will even- tually fall to pieces.

In addition, without the courage to seek to be ourselves, bad results are possible. Not only do we run the risk of missing our lives but also, in our egoism, we may seek to destroy others' lives and reputations as well. Bullying and electronically sending out personal attacks into the airwaves, for example, are acts of cowardice that can arise out of extreme narcissism or a failure to appreciate our own gifts. The person may fear or not recognize the need, in such cases, to truly look at themselves so they can see, acknowledge, and both embrace their wonderful gifts and recognize their shortcomings. Prejudice and racism also are the products of such anxieties, based on the failure to appreciate one's ordinary self to the extent that we can honor others who are different than we are, instead of submitting to a sense of "group think" with others who may also be insecure, narcissistic, or egoistic.

In his book, *On Desire: Why We Want What We Want*, William B. Irvine poses the following challenging question:

> Because fame requires the cooperation of other people, it puts us at the mercy of those same people. . . . How would our behavior change if other people vanished? It is only a slight exaggeration to say we live for other people—that the bulk of our time, energy, and wealth is spent creating and maintaining a certain public image of ourselves. . . . [Danish existentialist philosopher, poet, social critic and theologian] Søren Kierkegaard characterizes envy as failed admiration because the feelings are mixed with a sense of injustice [on our part].

Given this, the questions I have posed elsewhere in my writings[1] are as follows: How much energy would we save if unproductive comparisons were not part of our center of gravity? How much energy would then be available for us and those we co-journey with to simply enjoy life if comparisons were less and flowing with our life was more of a reality?

We also run the risk of mistaking the roles and labels we have when we are not aware of the core of who we are, our ordinary selves. In *The Tibetan Book of Living and Dying*, Sogyal Rinpoche poses the following question while keeping this point in mind: "We find that our identity depends entirely on an endless collection of things to prop it up: our name, our 'biography,' our partners, family, home, job, friends. . . . So when they are all taken away, will we have any idea of who we really are?"

In a similar vein, Richard Bode, in his simple but thought-provoking work, *First You Have to Row a Little Boat*, uses sailing as a metaphor for appreciating our own ordinary life for what it fully could be. As in the case of sailing, pointing to the need for attention to appreciating the winds of life, he suggests we "tack" through life by making the right adjustments as a sailor might in tacking his sloop, which turns out to be the most advantageous way of crossing a body of water instead of seeking to race directly ahead as others might. In his own words:

> The truth is that in our daily lives we constantly make similar migrations for land to water and back to land again—and we don't always do so with the fluency of a sailor. Time flips us rapidly from place to place and role to role. We shuttle from suburb to city, from home to job, from business meeting to

dinner party. Each milieu has its own conventions and makes its own demands. Sometimes the changes occur so fast we lose our bearings. We behave like parents to our colleagues and executives to our kids. We lack a sure sense of the appropriate because we haven't taken the time to figure out where we are.

Much of this wisdom arose from Bode's time sailing alone on his beloved sloop. Bode also had an accident that caused an added degree of forced idleness. During this period, he reflected:

> I thought deeply about who I was, where I came from, and what I wanted to be. What I had lost in physical motion I gained in insight, which is movement of another kind. I learned the interior life was as rewarding as the exterior life and that my richest moments occurred when I was absolutely still.

What he is pointing out here has been emphasized in the discussion earlier of alonetime (see Chapter 6). Such periods, though, must not be undertaken at a single point in our life but as we move through the different transitions and ages of our life.

Ordinariness can appear at every stage of life, starting maybe especially in childhood. When we encounter it, we can truly feel the joy of the spontaneity, transparency, and straightforward honesty of the young so often lost starting in adolescence and then to a greater degree in adulthood. As I type these words, I am reminded of a story a friend of mine told me about someone in her family.

A young girl accompanied her sister who was an undergraduate at the university at which I taught. The occasion was "siblings weekend." The general goal for the weekend event was to have a child have an opportunity to spend time with her sister and also see what university life is like.

After the weekend was over, the university student's roommate smiled at the younger child and said, by way of seeking to pay her a compliment, "You are very precocious." At which point the older sister turned to her younger sibling and said, "You don't know what that means do you?" To which the younger sister nodded her head up and down to indicate that she indeed did know what it meant.

The older sister frowned and said with a smile, "Well, what does it mean?"

At which point, the young girl, paused for a moment and said, "It means that I know things at my age that I shouldn't."

Hearing this, the older sister's eyes widened and she said, "How did you know that?"

To which her little sister replied, "Because I'm precocious!"[2]

In line with these simple, clear, and humorous interactions, *The Tao of Ordinariness: Humility and Simplicity in a Narcissistic Age* asks us: Are we willing to embrace ordinariness at the age we are now and as we move forward in life? As children, most of us were—in a very unadorned, unabashed way—our unvarnished selves. We probably flowed out of our personality style and interacted with others simply, clearly, and with an expectation that others would as well. Now, as adults, we tend to wrap ourselves up in our own often unexamined thinking and believe it to be equal to "the total truth" until someone pokes a hole in it, possibly with the aid of exaggeration or humor.

Humor at times is the best way to help us open up and be released from our own small cognitive envelope so we can gain a new perspective on ourselves and the world. It can also in very real ways help us to uncover in ourselves and others the hidden negatives that we sometimes harbor in our hearts and minds. For example, when I am annoyed or a bit depressed I often exaggerate things to draw out and demonstrate the nonsense that is sitting destructively just below the surface of my awareness. I also tease others in the same way when I feel that is what is going on with them as well. Since I do it in a way that is so hyperbolic, they realize what I am doing, and we can laugh together at the distorted, partially hidden belief that they, as well as I at times, so easily embrace.

Once a former classmate who is now a Catholic priest called me to ask if he might come over for dinner. As we sat relaxing before sitting down to eat, he mentioned that he was a bit down because of his work the past six years as a vocation director. He told me about the difficulties of the work, how other priests in his society couldn't understand the nature of his work. He went on to say that he felt his goal wasn't simply to "get more bodies" into their group but more importantly to help the people who were thinking about priesthood to discern more clearly what they felt God was calling them to do in life. That was his real job.

In response, I asked, "Well, in the six years you have done this work, how many new candidates for the priesthood in your society have you gotten?"

Hearing this, he made a face and responded, "You are so crass, Bob. 'How many have you gotten?' What a question to ask. The numbers aren't important. My work involves helping people discern what their future roles in life will be. If they wish to become priests, fine. If not, fine."

I pushed on. "Jim, how many have you gotten?"

He said a little exasperated now, "You just don't understand. Numbers aren't the issue, Bob. It's more than that."

I finally said, "Jim, stop equivocating; in the past six years how many have you gotten?"

To which he replied in a low voice, "None."

"None!" I said. "Well, no wonder you feel the way you do, you should be depressed. You are a *total* failure!"

Knowing me, Jim's eyes widened, and he responded while laughing loudly, "Boy, am I glad I came to see you for help! People pay you for this?"

After we laughed a bit over my outrageousness, he was able to speak in more detail about how, without realizing it, he had absorbed the sense of failure others felt about the lack of priestly vocations in the Catholic church. He could see that although he was saying the right things and was fulfilling an important guiding role in young men's lives, he was believing something else without recognizing it. This was causing him more pain than he had realized.

The same can be said when we verbally acclaim that we seek to embrace humility and simplicity, release the unhelpful influences around us, and resist going down the psychological *cul de sac* of egoism but still feel very much within us the disapproval of others when we don't "measure up" to their stated and unstated wishes for us.

Humor can help us face unhelpful expectations of others that will lead us in a direction not suited for our personality, ethics, and the mission in life that we feel called to because of our talents and our vision of what a full life would be like, given who we believe we are. Too often we allow ourselves to get pulled into situations that may even be positive ones and are good on the face of it, but without any sense of our own goals, reasonable needs, and limits. I think this is what Rev. Edward Jeffrey was thinking when he wrote in the June 14, 1964 issue of the *Observer* that "people expect the clergy to have the grace of a swan, the friendliness of a sparrow, the strength of an eagle, and the night hours of an owl—and some people expect such a bird to live on the food of a canary."

For many of us, living with our unexamined expectations of ourselves—as well as those of others in our interpersonal network—without questioning them or our view of ourselves prevents us from living more authentically and with greater freedom. Too often the image we have of ourselves has been wrought early in life, and we continue to move through our daily, weekly, monthly, and yearly activities as if on automatic pilot. Then we complain, "Where did the time go?" My oldest brother Ron once asked my father whether his sixty-eight years went by fast. My father, who was sitting in the back yard of our Queens home at the time with his legs propped up on a railing leading up from the basement, looked at him, snapped his fingers, and said in a soft voice, "Just like that."

We can't prevent time from moving along. We can't avoid the natural presence of expectations and views of ourselves—both unreasonable and sensible. But we can have a better sense of identity that is more impervious to who the outside world may inappropriately demand us to be. In the spirit of the quite different images of "the pearl" and "the opal,"[3] one of this book's goals is to move us away from "the unobtainable pearl" as an image for our identity—even though this may have been given to us by any number of outside forces from family to culture, in literature or from religion. Instead, the search for our ordinariness, I believe, is more a journey in seeking "the opal" of ordinariness—one in which there are many facets, some very visible and others almost hidden, until the light of our appreciation lets them come into view—for ourselves and others.

Such a recognition makes living our ordinary lives a greater possibility in the time we have left. We truly seek to embrace D. H. Lawrence's words, "Below what we think we are we are something else, we are almost anything." As I move through the final phase of my own life, I believe this more than ever before. Whereas I grasped the pearl of enthusiasm and passion that have been hallmarks of my work in supervising, mentoring, teaching, and serving as a therapist to professional helpers and healers, I now seek to embrace more fully the opal of myself. Gentleness, patience, a listening spirit, and kindness all seem more important now. And, as I give them more light, they have a better opportunity to shine more clearly through my personality and help my passion to be shared as a warmer light than in the past.

This insight and behavior have caused some sadness for me because as I focus more on a gentle form of passion, I see more and more how I failed to be kind in the past and now in the present. Yet, this sadness doesn't detract from my seeking a more robust ordinariness that reflects my failures in being a more balanced person. Instead, it excites me that, even now as I move past seventy years of age, there is unlearning and new learning in the air. There is the crackle of yet a new adventure in life that would not have been possible in my earlier years. I just was not ready—or, to be honest, really interested. How lucky I am that I am interested *now*.

Without attention to the humility, simplicity, courage, reflective time, and possible mentoring needed to appreciate who we are in an unvarnished way, we run the risk of remaining observers of a life that seems like ours. Without an awareness of ordinariness in deeper, more compelling ways, we may simply wander in a fog of "oughts," roles, others' needs, and shame if we step out of line. However, with a greater sensitivity to how the virtue of ordinariness can be lived out more fully in our lives, we can change all that. We can return home to our self *again*. But this time, it will be with eyes that can see it more clearly and live it out in the freshness of childhood with the wisdom of maturity. What a rewarding vision that can be, if we take the time, energy, courage, and *silent periods*, so rare today, to attend to what is going on within and around us. As Michel Foucault, in his work *Politics, Philosophy, and Culture*, aptly noted in 1988:

> I think silence is one of these things that has unfortunately been dropped from our culture. We don't have a culture of silence. . . . Young Romans or young Greeks were taught to keep silent in very different ways according to the people with whom they were interacting. Silence was then a specific form of experiencing a relationship with others. This is something that I believe is really worth cultivating. I'm in favor of developing silence as an inner and outer cultural ethos.

As we reflect on the major themes underpinning the spirit of ordinariness that are contained in this book and may have been stirred up in your own mind and mirrored in your own experiences, albeit in unique ways, we begin to see that ordinariness is so much more than the world would have us believe. If we were to develop a personal retreat on the contents of this book, it might contain the following points to consider, in silence and in a discussion with a mentor or treasured friend: *Ordinariness is an attitude of living and of reflecting on ourselves in ways that seek to:*

- Embrace the true humility that comes from knowing our own gifts and appreciating our own growing edges, weakness, and challenges with a sense of equanimity.
- See life clearly as it is, not as we might wish it to be.
- Embrace the call to be who we might become while accepting where we are at the moment.
- Move toward accepting all of life—including sadness, questions to which we have no answers, and unwanted feelings and the thoughts and beliefs underpinning them that we haven't examined as fully as we should.
- Offer others the space to be themselves that we would want for ourselves.
- Question the reputation we currently have with ourselves so it can open up a larger and more accurate self-narrative that we are the author of rather than giving this responsibility over to society, family, history, past trauma, or unexamined rules.
- Find the crumbs of silence and solitude already present in our life so we can relish rather than seek to immediately fill them.
- Challenge the needs we say we have or the ones others say we *must* fill in order to be happy.
- Value pacing and timeliness over haste.
- Become more aware of what we are experiencing in the present moment rather than jumping to conclusions and unnecessary judgments.

- Honor a spirit of "unlearning" so that we can be our ordinary self in the now rather than be captured by what we learned that was helpful in the past but doesn't apply to us today.
- Reject an egoistic way of viewing the world as revolving only around us.
- Avoid comparisons with others that are not helpful.
- Gain a more appropriate sense of transparency that comes from being a person without guile so we can help psychologically and spiritually purify the inner and interpersonal environment as much as is possible.
- Examine the conversations we have with ourselves to see how accurate and helpful they are so that when they aren't we can begin to entertain more helpful alternate stories about our life that will encourage and challenge us in good ways.
- Have other truly ordinary models accompany us on our journey while maintaining a willingness to open up a similar interpersonal space for others.
- Categorize ourselves and others less so we can be open to understanding more deeply who we and others simply are— not who we and others are as others have categorized us.
- Celebrate our uniqueness and the difference of others and seek how they may be teaching us new ways of self-understanding and a more multifaceted appreciation of the world.
- Avoid the dangers of extreme self-doubt on the one hand and inordinate self-confidence on the other.
- Be more in touch with and able to self-regulate our emotions.

- Not waste energy on pleasing others but have a willingness to be compassionate and empathic without expecting anything in return.
- Recognize that becoming more aware of our own personality strengths and personal joyful pursuits is an essential and worthwhile undertaking.
- Desire not simply to "fix" what is wrong with ourselves but, more importantly, to build on the positive aspects of our ordinary self.
- Develop a mission statement and ethic of living that flows with an appreciation of our ordinary self, not simply the unexamined dictates of others—especially when fear or a sense of entitlement is in play in the environment or in ourselves.
- Examine the feedback we have received that was helpful as well as that which was off-putting.
- Enjoy being with ourselves and laughing at ourselves when we have egoistically become defensive, rather than letting ourselves be softened by what we have experienced.
- Appreciate which persons and situations make life more joyful and meaningful for us.
- Know better the signature strengths that we have so we can share them more effectively with others.
- Be aware of what we would like written on our epitaph.
- Develop an innate ability to be *intrigued* by our ordinary self, as we might be by someone we admire or find has a sense of simplicity, humility, inner freedom, and courageousness yet ordinariness about them.

In my previous work on the themes of resilience, self-care, compassion, and maintaining a healthy perspective, one of the general statements I made was as follows:

> As I look back over forty years of being a psychotherapist, mentor, and clinical supervisor of helping professionals, as well as in my reflection on the guidance I have received, there are questions that I wished I could have or would have asked. Surprisingly for me, they are almost all about one thing: *releasing* or what many term "letting go."
>
> Maybe I didn't ask such questions, because in pacing the session, they didn't seem appropriate. Possibly as I walked with persons on a turn in their professional or personal life journey, I felt the question would ask too much—and maybe that was true at the time. Or in my own life, the questions may not have surfaced because I was afraid of where they might lead. No matter what the reason, the end result was the same: less inner freedom and a failure to fully fathom the amazing paradox of letting go.[4]

While I think this is certainly true, today I would refine my belief to read: The most important thing we can do for ourselves and the world around us is releasing what is not of us so we can enjoy our ordinary selves and share ourselves freely with others. That is what I believe the import of this book and the summative points just made are about. Certainly, I believe ordinariness is relevant in our times—especially given the number of persons suffering from egoism and narcissism who have taken on leadership roles in many venues of our society and are, whether we like it or not, models for our children. The time for rediscovery of the virtue of ordinariness by all of us is *now*. Paradoxically, this virtue can help us to be so much more than we are now, *if* we begin to value and explore it anew as individuals and as a society.

NOTES

Epigraph

1. This comment by Ajahn Chah was quoted by Jack Kornfield.

Chapter One

1. This story is one I have used in my presentations because it makes the point that humility is not something we can be guaranteed even if we desire it. The story appeared in both my books *No Problem* and *Night Call*.

2. A slightly different version of this story appears in print in Anthony de Mello's delightful collection of interactions between a master and a disciple, entitled *One Minute Wisdom*.

Chapter Two

1. Shin Ling, "Is A Buddhist Group Changing China or Being Changed?" *New York Times*, June 25, 2017, International section, pp. 1, 15.

Chapter Three

1. These were originally discussed in my now out-of-print book, *Seeds of Sensitivity*.

Chapter Four

1. In my book *Bounce*, this topic is explored further.
2. Jessica Bennett, "Learning to Fail," *New York Times*, June 25, 2017, Lifestyle section, pp. 1, 2.

Chapter Five

1. Quoted in Millicent Dillon. *A Little Original Sin: The Life and Work of Jane Bowles*. Berkeley: University of California Press, 1981, p. 82.
2. Shunryu Suzuki. *Not Always So*. New York: Harper Collins, 2002, p. x.
3. Quoted in Joseph Telushkin. *Rebbe*. New York: Harper Collins, 2014.

Chapter Six

1. Henri J. M. Nouwen, "Foreword," *The Practice of the Presence of God*, Edited by John J. Delaney. New York: Doubleday, 1977, pp. 9, 10.
2. Hugh Delehanty, "Radical Kindness: Anne Lamott—The Mindfulness Interview," *Mindful*, June 2017, pp. 68–71.

Epilogue

1. Robert J. Wicks. *The Inner Life of the Counselor*. Hoboken, NJ: Wiley, 2012, p. 164.

2. I am grateful to Eloise Wilding for sharing this personal story with me.

3. I am grateful to Brendan Geary for sharing with me a passage from the book, *The Opal and the Pearl*, by Mark Patrick Hederman, in which these images appear, from a letter that James Joyce wrote to his friend Nora on August 21, 1909.

4. Robert J. Wicks. *Night Call: Embracing Compassion and Hope in a Troubled World*. New York: Oxford University Press, 2018, pp. 121, 122.

SOURCES CITED

Alain (Émile-August Chartres) *Propos Sur le Bonheur* (Paris: Gallimard, 1998).

Bakewell, Sarah *At the Existentialist Café* (New York: Other Press, 2016).

Beston, Henry *The Outermost House* (New York: St. Martin's Press, 1928).

Bode, Richard *First You Have to Row a Little Boat* (New York: Grand Central, 1993).

Brazier, David *Zen Therapy* (Hoboken, NJ: Wiley, 1995).

Brooks, David *Road to Character* (New York: Random House, 2015).

Brown, David S. *Paradise Lost: A Life of F. Scott Fitzgerald* (Cambridge, MA: Harvard University Press, 2017).

Byrd, William *Alone* (New York: Kodansha, 1995).

Canetti, Elias *Notes from Hampstead* (New York: Farrar, Straus and Giroux, 1998).

Chadwick, David *The Crooked Cucumber* (New York: Broadway, 1999).

Conroy, Pat *A Lowcountry Heart* (New York: Doubleday, 2016).

Conroy, Pat *My Reading Life* (New York: Doubleday, 2010).

Crane, George *Bones of the Master* (New York: Bantam, 2000).

cummings, e. e. *e.e. cummings, A Miscellany,* edited by George James Firmage (London: Owen, 1965).

Dalai Lama *My Spiritual Journey* (San Francisco: Harper One, 2009).

Dalai Lama and Tutu, Desmond, with Douglas Abrams *The Book of Joy* (New York: Avery, 2016).

de Mello, Anthony *One Minute Wisdom* (New York: Doubleday, 1986).

Dillard, Annie *The Writing Life* (New York: Harper Perennial, 1989).

Dillon, Millicent *A Little Original Sin* (Los Angeles: University of California Press, 1998).

Epstein, Mark *The Trauma of Everyday Life* (New York: Penguin, 2013).

Foucault, Michel *Politics, Philosophy & Culture* (New York: Routledge, 2015).

France, Peter *Hermits* (New York: St. Martin's Press, 1996).

France, Peter *Patmos* (New York: Atlantic Monthly Press, 2002).

Frankl, Viktor *Man's Search for Meaning* (New York: Washington Square Press, 1984).

Fuller, R Buckminster cited in *Availability,* by Robert J. Wicks (Notre Dame: Sorin Books, 2015).

Gardner, Daniel *The Science of Fear* (New York: Dutton, 2008).

Georgiou, S.T. *The Way of the Dreamcatcher* (Ottawa: Novalis, 2002).

Gibran, Kahlil *Sand and Foam* (New York: Knopf, 1967).

Grumbach, Doris *Fifty Days of Solitude* (Boston: Beacon, 1999).

Harvey, Andrew *Journey in Ladakh* (Boston: Houghton Mifflin Company, 1983).

Hendricksen, Paul *Hemingway's Boat* (New York: Random House, 2011).

Hershey, Terry *The Power of Pause* (Chicago: Loyola Press, 2009).

Heschel, Abraham *Man is Not Alone. A Philosophy of Religion* (New York: Farrar, Straus and Giroux, 1951).

Heschel, Abraham *God in Search of Man* (New York: Farrar, Straus and Giroux, 1955).

Hoff, Benjamin *The Te of Piglet* (New York: Dutton, 1992).

Housden, Roger *Ten Poems to Change Your Life* (New York: Harmony, 2001).

Irvine, William *On Desire* (New York: Oxford University Press, 2005).

Iyer, Pico *The Open Road* (New York: Knopf, 2008).

James, Erwin "A Life Outside" (*The Guardian*, 30 September 2004).

James, Henry *Washington Square* (New York: Signet Classics, 1880/2004).

James, William quoted in *Pure Act,* by Michael McGregor (New York: Fordham University Press, 2016).

Johnson, Sandy *The Book of Tibetan Elders* (New York: Riverhead, 1996).

Jones, Alan *Soul Making* (San Francisco: Harper, 1985).

Joseph, Stephen *Authentic: How to be Yourself and Why It Matters* (London: Piatkus/Little Brown, 2016).

Jouard, Sidney *The Transparent Soul* (rev. ed.) (New York: Van Nostrand Reinhold, 1971).

Kagge, Erling *Silence* (New York: Pantheon Books, 2017).

Karr, Mary *The Art of Memoir* (New York: Harper Collins, 2015).

Kohut, Henry "Dynamic Psychotherapy and Its Frustrations," in *Resistance,* by Paul Wachtel (New York: Plenum, 1982, pp. 3–23).

Krishnamurti *Life Ahead* (New York: New World Library, 1901/2005).

Langewiesche *Sahara Unveiled* (New York: Random House, 1996).

Leary, Mark *The Curse of the Self* (New York: Oxford University Press, 2004).

Lee, Hermione *Biography* (Oxford: Oxford University Press).

Maitland, Sara *A Book of Silence* (Berkeley, CA: Counterpoint, 2008).

Matthiessen, Peter *Nine Headed Dragon* (Boston: Shambhala, 1986).

McGregor, Michael *Pure Act: The Uncommon Life of Robert Lax* (New York: Fordham University Press, 2016).

Merton, Thomas *A Vow of Conversation* (New York: Farrar, Straus, and Giroux, 1988).

Merton, Thomas *My Argument with the Gestapo* (New York: Doubleday, 1969).

Merton, Thomas *The Sign of Jonas* (New York: Doubleday, 1953).

Merton, Thomas *Thoughts in Solitude* (New York: Doubleday, 1968).

Merton, Thomas *Wisdom of the Desert* (New York: New Directions, 1960).

Milford, Nancy *Savage Beauty: The Life of Edna St. Vincent Millay* (New York: Random House, 2002).

Millman, Lawrence "Introduction," in *A Woman in the Polar Night*, by Christiane Ritter (Fairbanks, AK: University of Alaska Press, 2010).

Murdoch, Iris *The Sovereignty of Good* (London: Routledge, 2001).

Norris, Kathleen *Acedia and Me* (New York: Riverhead, 2008).

Nouwen, Henri *Way of the Heart* (New York: Seabury, 1981).

Palmer, Parker *Let Your Life Speak* (San Francisco: Jossey-Bass, 2000).

Penny, Louise *Glass Houses* (New York: Minotaur, 2017).

Prevallet, Elaine *Reflections on Simplicity* (Wallingford, PA: Pendle Hill Publications, 1982).

Ricard, Matthieu *Happiness* (Boston: Little Brown: 2003).

Rilke, Ranier Maria *Letters to a Young Poet* (New York: Norton, 1934).

Ritter, Christiane *A Woman in the Polar Night* (Fairbanks, AK: University of Alaska, 2010).

Saint-Exupéry, Antoine *The Little Prince* (New York: Harcourt Brace and Company, 1943).

Sanford, John *Healing and Wholeness* (Mahwah, NJ: Paulist Press, 1977).

Schneider, Pat *Writing Alone and with Others* (New York: Oxford University Press).

Steindl-Rast, David *Gratefulness, the Heart of Prayer* (Mahwah, NJ: Paulist Press, 1984).

Storr, Anthony *Solitude* (New York: Ballantine, 1988).

Strand, Clark *The Wooden Bowl* (New York: Hyperion, 1998).

Stril-Rever, Sofia, "Forward," in *My Spiritual Journey*, by the Dalai Lama (San Francisco: Harper One, 2009).

Suzuki, Shunryu *To Shine One Corner of the World*, edited by David Chadwick (New York: Broadway, 2001).

Telushkin, Joseph *Rebbe* (New York: Harper Wave, 2014).

Twain, Mark *Innocents Abroad* (New York: Oxford University Press, 1996).

Twain, Mark *Puddin' Head Wilson* (New York: Vintage, 2015).

Untermeyer, Louis quoted in *Savage Beauty: The Life of Edna St Vincent Millay*, by Nancy Mitford (New York: Random House, 2001).

Walls, Laura Dassow *Henry David Thoreau: A Life* (Chicago: University of Chicago Press, 2017).

Wehner, Peter "The Power of Humility" (*New York Times*, April 16, 2017).

White, Michael and Epston, David *Narrative Means to Therapeutic Ends* (New York: Norton, 1990).

Whitman, Walt "Song of Myself," in *Leaves of Grass* (London: Walter Scott, 1836).

Wicks, Robert J. *Bounce: Living the Resilient Life* (New York: Oxford University Press, 2010).

Wicks, Robert J. *Crossing the Desert* (Notre Dame: Sorin Books, 2007).

Wicks, Robert J. *Night Call: Embracing Compassion and Hope in a Troubled World.* (New York: Oxford University Press, 2018).

Wicks, Robert J. *Perspective: The Calm within the Storm* (New York: Oxford University Press, 2014).

Wicks, Robert J. *Touching the Holy* (Notre Dame: Sorin Books, 2007).

Woolf, Virginia *Collected Essays*, edited by L. Woolf (London: Catto and Windus, 1966–7).

ABOUT THE AUTHOR

For over 35 years, Robert Wicks has been called to speak calm into chaos to individuals and groups experiencing great stress, anxiety, and confusion. Dr. Wicks received his doctorate in psychology from Hahnemann Medical College and Hospital, is Professor Emeritus at Loyola University Maryland, and has taught in universities and professional schools of psychology, medicine, nursing, theology, education, and social work. In 2003 he was the commencement speaker for Wright State School of Medicine in Dayton, Ohio, and in 2005 he was both visiting scholar and the commencement speaker at Stritch School of Medicine in Chicago. He also was commencement speaker at and recipient of honorary doctorates from both Georgian Court University and Caldwell College in New Jersey.

In the past several years he has spoken on Capitol Hill to members of Congress and their chiefs of staff; at Johns Hopkins School of Medicine, the U.S. Air Force Academy, the Mayo Clinic, the North American Aerospace Defense Command, and the Defense Intelligence Agency; at Harvard's Children's Hospital and Harvard Divinity School, Yale School of Nursing, and Princeton Theological Seminary; and to members of the NATO Intelligence Fusion Center in England on his major areas of expertise: resilience, self-care, and the prevention of secondary stress (the pressures encountered in reaching out to others). He has also spoken at the Boston Public Library's commemoration of the Boston Marathon bombing; addressed 10,000 educators in the Air Canada Arena in Toronto; given the opening keynote speech to 1,500 physicians of the American Medical Directors Association; spoken at the FBI and New York City Police and Correctional Academies; led a course on re-silience in Beirut for relief workers from Aleppo, Syria; and addressed caregivers in China, Vietnam, India, Thailand, Haiti, Northern Ireland, Scotland, Hungary, Guatemala, Malta, New Zealand, Australia, France, England, and South Africa.

In 1994, he was responsible for the psychological debriefing of relief workers evacuated from Rwanda during the genocide. In 1993 and again in 2001, he worked in Cambodia. During these visits, his work was with professionals from the English-speaking community who were there to help the Khmer people rebuild their nation following years of terror and torture. In 2006 he delivered presentations on self-care at the National

Naval Medical Center in Bethesda, Maryland, and at Walter Reed Army Hospital to health care professionals responsible for the care of Iraq and Afghan war veterans evacuated to the United States with multiple amputations and severe head injuries. More recently he addressed U.S. Army health care professionals returning from Africa, where they were assisting during the Ebola crisis.

Dr. Wicks has published over 50 books both for professionals and for the general public, including the bestselling *Riding the Dragon*. His latest books from Oxford University Press for a general readership are *Night Call: Embracing Compassion and Hope in a Troubled World*, *Perspective: The Calm within the Storm*, and *Bounce: Living the Resilient Life*. Two of his latest books for professionals include *Overcoming Secondary Stress in Medical and Nursing Practice* and *The Resilient Clinician*. His books have been translated into Chinese, Korean, Indonesian, Polish, and Spanish. In 2006, Dr. Wicks received the first annual Alumni Award for Excellence in Professional Psychology from Widener University, and he is the recipient of the Humanitarian of the Year Award from the American Counseling Association's Division on Spirituality, Ethics and Religious Values in Counseling. Dr. Wicks also served as a U.S. Marine Corps officer.

INDEX

Abbas, 35, 174

Abraham (biblical figure), 47–48

Abrams, Douglas, 49

acceptance, 8, 30, 89–91, 197

Acedia and Me (Norris), 35

adolescence, 6, 111

advertising, 12, 16, 136–37

After the Ecstasy, The Laundry (Kornfield), 77–79, 149

Alain (Émile-August Chartres), 53

Alone (Byrd), 176–77

alonetime, 9, 36–37, 164–84, 189

  author's experience of, 164–68

  benefits of for embracing ordinariness, 182–83

  darkness met with, 106–7

  defined, 36, 169–70

emotional maturity and, 177–78

fantasy and, 171–72

meditation and, 171, 172–74, 177–78, 179, 181

without physical separation, 180

places and people of, 175–84

aluminum pot anecdote, 12–14

Ammas, 35, 174

Angelou, Maya, 120, 153

antisocial disorders, 31–32

Appleton, William, 81–82

Arche, L', 162

Argument with the Gestapo (Merton), 137

arrogance, 119–20

"Art of Gracious Leadership, The" (Brooks), 26–27

Art of Memoir, The (Karr), 153–54

asceticism, 56–57
At the Existentialist Café (Bakewell),
    5, 89–90
Augustine of Hippo, 49–50
Authentic: How to Be Yourself and Why It
    Matters (Joseph), 7, 80–81, 148
authenticity, 7, 114
    alonetime and, 183
    vs. darkness, 107–8
    fame valued over, 7–8
    mentors in ordinariness and,
        153, 157

Bakewell, Sarah, 5, 89–90
Bankei, 124
Bantu tribesmen, 2
Basch, Michael Franz, 85–86
Beck, Aaron T., 117–18
Beginning Mindfulness (Weiss), 181
Bennett, Jessica, 129–30, 204n7
Beston, Henry, 1
Bird by Bird (LaMotte), 184
bittul ha-yesh, 148–49
Bode, Richard, 188–89
Bones of the Master (Crane), 59–60
Book of Joy, The (Dalai Lama and Tutu),
    37, 38, 49, 142
Book of Silence, A (Maitland), 168
Book of Tibetan Elders, The (Johnson),
    142, 171–72
Bounce (Wicks), 98, 204n6
Bowles, Jane, 112, 138
Brackett, Elder, 53
Bramacari, 100–1
Brazier, David, 112–13, 139–40

Brooks, David, 18–19, 39–40
    "The Art of Gracious
        Leadership," 26–27
    The Road to Character, 18–19, 186
Brown, David S., 65
Buber, Martin, 8
Buddha, 80, 118
Buddhism, 3–4, 12, 50–51, 118, 179
    in China, 63–65
    Zen, 40
bullying, 186–87
Bush, George W., 29–30
Byrd, William, 176–77

Cameroonian proverb, 138–39
Camus, Albert, 116
Canetti, Elias, 71–72
Catholic Worker Movement, 140, 141
Chadwick, David, 40–42, 171
Chah, Ajahn, 203n1
change, 155
character disorders. *See* personality/
    character disorders
Chardin, Pierre de, 118
charis, 146
Chartres, Émile-August, 53
cheerleader voice/friend, 144
childhood, 2, 10, 189–91
China, 34–35, 63–65
Chocano, Carina, 33–34
Chödrön, Pema, 134–36
Christianity, 27–28, 50–51
City of God (Augustine), 49–50
Clinton, Hillary, 26
Coles, Robert, 140–41

common sense, 57–58
compassion, 9, 36–37, 51, 200
  ego-less, 158–59
  self-, 44–45
confirmation bias, 47
Conroy, Pat, 138
courage, 9, 76–77, 79, 114, 115–16,
  121, 128, 179, 185–86, 195–96
Crane, George, 59–60
criticism, 77, 86, 91–96
  author's experiences of, 93–94, 95
  impurity of, 92
  opportunities provided by, 92–93
  The Te of Piglet on, 126–27
Crooked Cucumber, The (Chadwick), 40–41
Crouse, Karen, 24–25
cummings, e. e., 2–3, 17–18
Cure of the Self, The (Leary), 43–44

Dalai Lama, 10–11, 51
  The Book of Joy, 37, 38, 49, 142
  humility of, 37–38
  as a mentor in ordinariness, 142–43
  simplicity of, 54–55
Dangerfield, Rodney, 117–18
darkness. *See* personal darkness
Day, Dorothy, 140–41
defense, uncovering subtle styles
  of, 72–79
Deh Chun, 55–56
Delehanty, Hugh, 204n12
de Mello, Anthony, 23, 46–47,
  203n3
desert metaphor, 58
desert monks, 35–36, 174

detachment, 62–63, 178–79
Dillard, Annie, 154–55
Dillon, Millicent, 112, 204n8
discouragement, 119–20
discovery, 128–29. *See also* self-discovery
Dixon, Trudy, 114
Drabble, Margaret, 80
Dragon River (Matthiessen), 96–97
Dunn, Irina, 109–10
"Dynamic Psychotherapy and Its
  Frustrations" (Basch), 85–86

egoism, 43–45, 116–17, 118,
  198, 200–1
  compassion without, 158–59
  failure and, 132, 134
  fear and, 129
  harming others and, 186–87
  humor vs., 117, 193
  mentors in ordinariness vs., 148–49,
    153, 156, 158–59, 161
  Ramakrishna on, 23
  Suzuki on, 42–43
ego skepticism, 44
Eigen, Michael, 120
Einstein, Albert, 16, 130
empathy., 29–30
Empire Strikes Back, The (film), 105–6
energy conservation, 123, 187–88
epitaph, 126, 199
Epstein, Mark, 12–14, 118–19, 120
Erickson, Erik, 111
Ethics and Public Policy Center, 27
eulogy virtues, 19
extra-ordinariness, 2, 25, 126–27, 159

failure, 14, 111, 114, 115–17
  dealing with, 129–34
  humor and, 132–34
  inevitability of, 130
  information on egoism from, 132, 134
  most painful aspect of, 130–31
fame, 7–8, 187
Faulkner, Robert, 138
fear, 15, 67, 115–16, 122, 128
  egoism and, 129
  encountering, 134–37
  as a marketing tactic, 136–37
  misplaced, 136–37
feedback, 86, 199
Ficke, Arthur, 98–99
Fifty Days of Solitude (Grumbach), 178–79
First You Have to Row a Little Boat (Bode), 188–89
Fitzgerald, F. Scott, 65–66
Fogel, Robert, 136
Fo Guang Shan, 64
forgiveness, 51, 77–79
Foucault, Michel, 195–96
"fox mind," 60
France, Peter, 35, 146, 175
Frankl, Viktor, 185
freedom, 123
  alonetime and, 179
  sense of self and, 96–97
  simplicity and, 72
friendship, 148
Fuller, Alexandra, 123, 151–52
Fuller, R. Buckminster, 15–16

Gardner, Daniel, 47, 136–37
Geary, Brendan, 205n15
General Theological Seminary, 11
Genesee Diary, The (Nouwen), 166–67
Georgiou, S. T., 70–71, 102–3, 145–46
Gibran, Kahlil, 128
gifts, 14, 125, 126–27, 197
  alonetime and, 183
  failure to appreciate, 186–87
  humility and, 30, 49–50
  as problems, 116–17
  sense of self and, 88, 94–95
  simplicity and, 54, 57
Glass Houses (Penny), 31–32
God in Search of Man (Heschel), 150, 160
Good Man Is Hard to Find, A (O'Connor), 7–8
Graham, Billy, 141–42
Gratefulness, the Heart of Prayer (Steindl-Rast), 158
group polarization, 47
Grumbach, Doris, 178–79
Guardian, The, 175

Hahnemann Medical College, 95
Hammarskjöld, Dag, 128
Happiness (Ricard), 34–35, 56, 97, 172–73
harasser/teaser voice/friend, 144
Harvey, Andrew, 60–61, 144–45
Healing and Wholeness (Sanford), 17
Hederman, Mark Patrick, 205n15
Hemingway, Ernest, 97
Hemingway's Boat (Hendrickson), 115–16
Hendrickson, Paul, 115–16
Henry David Thoreau: A Life (Walls), 45

Hershey, Terry, 185
Heschel, Abraham Joshua, 52,
   150, 159–60
   God in Search of Man, 150, 160
   The Insecurity of Freedom, 160
   Man Is Not Alone, 159–60
   Questions Man Asks, 159
   The Sabbath, 164
Hiawatha, 87
Hoff, Benjamin, 126–27
honesty, 36, 105, 114, 183
Horowitz, Vladimir, 143
Housden, Roger, 6–7
humility, 9, 18–19, 23–52, 54, 55, 60,
   61, 64–65, 72, 115–16, 123,
   156, 193, 195–96, 197
   alonetime and, 183
   author's experience of, 38–39
   derivation of word, 35
   distorted use of concept, 33–35
   elusiveness of, 24, 39–45, 54
   fame valued over, 7–8
   humor and, 38
   politics lacking in, 25–30
   sense of self and, 88
   shunning of, 24
   spiritual figures modeling, 37–38
   sports and, 24–25
   unlearning and (*See* unlearning)
humor, 183, 190–93
   vs. egoism, 117, 193
   for facing unhelpful expectations, 193
   about failure, 132–34
   humility and, 38
Hurricane Harvey, 29

ignorance, 46, 119–20
image, 43. *See also* self-image
imago Dei, 8
improvement, 103–4, 156–57
Inner Life of the Counselor, The (Wicks),
   204n13
Innocents Abroad (Twain), 128–29
Insecurity of Freedom, The
   (Heschel), 160
inspirational voice/friend, 144
intrigue. *See* self-intrigue
Irvine, William B., 187
"Is A Buddhist Group Changing
   China or Being Changed?"
   (Johnson), 204n4
Iyer, Pico, 37, 54–55

James, Erwin, 175–77
James, Henry, 99
James, William, 1
Japanese soldiers (World War
   II), 77–79
Jaspers, Karl, 67
Jeffrey, Edward, 193
Jesus Christ, 28
Jewish tale of the rabbi, 23–24
Johnson, Ian, 63–65
Johnson, Jenna, 28–30
Johnson, Sandy, 142, 143, 171–72
Jones, Alan, 69–70
Joseph, Stephen, 7, 80–81, 148
Jouard, Sidney, 81, 114–15, 170–71
Journey in Ladakh (Harvey),
   60–61, 144–45
Joyce, James, 205n15

Kagge, Erling, 168–69
Karr, Mary, 153–54
Keller, Helen, 153
kenosis, 9, 70
Kierkegaard, Søren, 35, 187
Kipling, Rudyard, 165
Kohut, Heinz, 85
Kornfield, Jack, 174, 183–84,
   203n1
   After the Ecstasy, The Laundry,
   77–79, 149
   The Wise Heart, 179
Krishnamurti, 1
Kübler-Ross, Elisabeth, 112

LaMotte, Anne, 10, 184
Langewiesche, William, 58
Latimer, Matt, 29–30
Lawrence, D. H., 194–95
Lax, Robert, 66
   on kenosis, 70–71
   as a mentor in ordinariness, 145–46
   Merton compared with, 100–3
"Learning to Fail" (Bennett),
   129–30, 204n7
Leary, Mark, 43–45
Leaving Before the Rains Come (Fuller),
   123, 151–52
Ledecky, Katie, 24–25
Letters to a Young Poet (Rilke), 4–5, 124
letting go, 62–63, 69, 200–1
Let Your Life Speak (Palmer), 30–31,
   67, 69
Levinas, Emmanuel, 89–90
Life Ahead (Krishnamurti), 1

Little Original Sin, A: The Life and Work of
   Jane Bowles (Dillon), 112, 204n8
Little Prince, The (Saint-Exupéry), 99–100
Living World, The (radio program), 35
Lorde, Audre, 80
love, 9, 36–37, 83
   concrete vs. abstract, 131–32
   self-disclosure and, 115
"Lying Low" (Chocano), 33–34

Maitland, Sara, 168, 180–81, 182
Man Is Not Alone (Heschel), 159–60
Man's Search for Inner Meaning
   (Frankl), 185
Maral, Gabriel, 67
masks, 3–4, 6
Matthiessen, Peter, 4, 17, 96–97
May, Rollo, 89
McGregor, Michael, 66, 100–2
meditation, 172–74, 177–78, 181
   facing the questions of life
      with, 179
   simplicity of, 55
   Zazen, 41–42, 156, 171
mentors in ordinariness, 3–4, 9, 95–96,
   126–27, 138–63, 195–96
   avoiding impersonation of, 143,
      144–45, 151–53
   desirable traits in, 147–48
   inspiration and support
      from, 138–39
   unpretentiousness of, 145–46
   the words and themes of wisdom
      figures, 150–63
   "mentors of the moment," 162

Merton, Thomas, 16, 17, 112,
    152, 179–80
  Argument with the Gestapo, 137
  Lax compared with, 100–3
  Seven Story Mountain, 179–80
  A Vow of Conversation, 15, 164
  Wisdom of the Desert, 174
Millay, Edna St. Vincent, 80,
    98–99, 138–39
Millman, Lawrence, 176
Mindful magazine, 10
mindfulness, 119–20, 179, 181
mirroring, 8, 29–30, 107, 114, 149
mission statement, 199
Mitford, Nancy, 98–99
Murdoch, Iris, 5
My Favorite Questions (Peale), 141–42

narcissism, 7–8, 25, 52, 89, 94–95,
    104, 186–87, 200–1
narrative
  alonetime and, 180–81
  changing or expanding, 98–105,
    110–11, 123
Newfoundlanders, 132–34
New York Times, 26, 27
New York Times Magazine, 33
Niebuhr, Reinhold, 144
Night Call (Wicks), 98, 203n2, 205n16
Nine Headed Dragon (Matthiessen), 4
noise, 169
nonjudgmental attitude, 6, 36, 81,
    103–4, 168
No Problem (Wicks), 203n2
Norris, Kathleen, 35

Not Always So (Suzuki), 155, 204n9
Notes from Hampstead (Canetti), 71–72
Nouwen, Henri J. M., 164, 165–68,
    204n11

Observer, 193
O'Connor, Flannery, 7–8
Olmsted, Chris, 24–25
On Desire: Why We Want What We Want
    (Irvine), 187
One Minute Wisdom (de Mello),
    23, 203n3
Opal and the Pearl, The (Hederman), 205n15
"opal" image, 194–95
Open Road, The (Iyer), 37
ordinariness. *See also* alonetime; humility;
    mentors in ordinariness; sense of
    self; simplicity
  accomplishing, 5–6
  amazing experience of, 1
  benefits of reclaiming, 122–23
  consequences of not
    appreciating, 185–87
  as countercultural, 7–8, 104
  creative work and, 4–5
  differing processes for reaching, 66
  at every stage of life, 189–91
  as an evolution of the self, 16–17
  extra-, 2, 25, 126–27, 159
  getting lost in the search for, 14–15
  goals of living with, 196–99
  impact of addressing the virtue
    of, 10–12
  importance and difficulty of
    embracing, 114–16

ordinariness (*cont.*)
    inner obstacles to, 67
    as a lost/forgotten virtue, 1, 2–3,
        54, 184
    methods of achieving, 14
    outside influences *vs.*, 6–7
    perception of reality and, 117–18
    as a precarious undertaking, 104
    questions opening the way
        for, 125–26
    situations faced on journey to, 120–21
    spiritual search for, 3–4
    valuing with intention and
        determination, 2–3
other, the, 6, 31
Outermost House, The (Beston), 1

Palmer, Parker, 30–31, 67, 69
Paradise Lost: A Life of F. Scott Fitzgerald
    (Brown), 65
patience, 114, 115–16, 123
Patmos: A Place of Healing (France), 35,
    146, 175
"Peacemaker" (Iroquois tale), 87
Peale, Norman Vincent, 141–42
"pearl" image, 194–95
Penny, Louise, 31–32
perseverance, 9, 114, 123
personal darkness, 104–5, 125
    alonetime and, 106–7
    benefits of facing, 116–17
    mentoring and, 147
    narrative and, 110–11
    questions about, 107–9
    unnecessary, 105–11

personality/character disorders,
    31–32, 72–79
Perspective (Wicks), 98
politics, 25–30
Politics, Philosophy, and Culture
    (Foucault), 195–96
positive paradox, 88
positive psychology, 8, 38–39, 125
Posner, Salman, 148–49
Pound, Ezra, 168
Power of Praise, The (Hershey), 185
prejudice, 109–10, 186–87
Prevallet, Elaine, 53–54, 62–63
pride, 34–35, 140
"Profession for Women" (Woolf), 85
prophet voice/friend, 144
pruning, 93, 166
"psychological clothes," comfort
    in, 66–72
psychology/psychotherapy, 12, 179
    mentoring in, 139–40
    ordinariness valued in, 7–8, 117–18
    positive, 8, 38–39, 125
    self-, 85
    sense of self and, 81, 85–86, 95–96
    simplicity and, 69, 72–79
psychopaths, 31–32
Pudd'nhead Wilson (Twain), 128
Pure Act: The Uncommon Life of Robert Lax
    (McGregor), 100–2

Questions Man Asks (Heschel), 159
"Quiet Power of Humility, The"
    (Wehner), 27–28
Quindlen, Anna, 185

racism, 186–87

Radical Devotion, A (Coles), 140–41

"Radical Kindness: Ann Lamott—
The Mindfulness Interview"
(Delehanty), 204n12

Ramakrishna, 23

Reading Life, The (Conroy), 138

Rebbe (Telushkin), 148–49, 204n10

Reflections on Simplicity (Prevallet),
53–54, 62–63

reputation with yourself, 81–82, 197.
See also sense of self

resilience, 123, 133, 200

résumé virtues, 19

Ricard, Matthieu, 34–35, 56,
97, 172–73

Rilke, Ranier Maria, 4–5, 124

Rinpoche, Sogyal, 188

Ritter, Christine, 176–77

Road to Character, The (Brooks),
18–19, 186

Roth, Geneen, 184

Sabbath, The (Heschel), 164

Sahara Unveiled (Langewiesche), 58

Saint-Exupéry, Antoine de, 99–100

Saltza, Chris von. *See* Olmsted, Chris

Sand and Foam (Gibran), 128

Sanford, John, 17

Sarah (biblical figure), 47–48

Sartre, Jean Paul, 67

Savage Beauty (Mitford), 98–99

Sayers, Peig, 139

Schneerson, Menachem Mendel,
148–49, 161–62

Schneider, Pat, 15, 150–51

Schweitzer, Albert, 138

Science of Fear, The (Gardner), 47, 136–37

sea-kindliness, 115–16. *See also* courage;
failure; patience; perseverance

Seeds of Sensitivity (Wicks), 204n5

self-acceptance, 89–91, 120

self-appreciation, 88–89, 125

self-awareness, 118, 135–36

self-compassion, 44–45

self-disclosure, 81, 115–16

self-discovery, 120, 129, 177

self-esteem, 90–91, 109–10, 141
accurate, 88–89
criticism and, 93–95
defined, 88
humility and, 43
influences on, 84, 85–86
narcissistic baggage in, 94–95

self-image
arriving at, 83–87
over-concern with, 117
simplicity and, 71

self-intrigue, 119–20, 123, 126–27,
182, 199

self-psychology, 85

self-realization, 177

self-reflection, 43–44, 86

self-regulation, 198

self-respect, 94–96

Seligman, Martin, 125

sense of self, 80–111
accurate self-appreciation and space
for others in, 88–89
arriving at, 83–87

sense of self (*cont.*)
  darkness and (*See* personal darkness)
  exploring the unrecognizable
    you, 89–97
  narrative in (*See* narrative)
Seven Story Mountain (Merton), 179–80
sexual abuse, 121
Shin Ying, 63–65
signature strengths, 38–39, 99,
    116–17, 199
significant others, 83, 84, 114
silence, 165–70, 178, 195–96, 197
  courage needed for, 179
  impact on personal
    narrative, 180–81
Silence (Kagge), 168–69
simplicity, 9, 18–19, 52, 53–79,
    115–16, 123, 193, 195–96
  alonetime and, 182, 183
  kenosis and, 70
  letting go and, 62–63, 69
  travelling lightly and (*See* travelling
    lightly)
  wistful view of, 54, 59
"Simplicity and Ordinariness: The
    Climate of Early Cistercian
    Hagiography" (Waddell), 71–72
solitude, 165–68, 169–71, 197
  courage needed for, 179
  impact on personal narrative, 180–81
  people and places associated with,
    176, 177–79
Solitude: A Return to the Self (Storr), 177
Song of Myself (Whitman), 53
Soul Making (Jones), 69–70

sports, 24–25
St. Michael's College, 164–65, 167–68
Stein, Gertrude, 97
Steindl-Rast, David, 158–59
Storr, Edwin, 177
Strand, Clark, 55–56, 173
Suzuki, Shunryu, 103, 171
  humility of, 40–43, 48, 156
  as a mentor in ordinariness, 139,
    152–53, 155–57
  Not Always So, 155, 204n9
  ordinariness of, 114
  To Shine One Corner of the World, 41–42

Telushkin, Joseph, 148–49, 204n10
Ten Poems to Change Your Life
    (Housden), 6–7
Te of Piglet, The (Hoff), 126–27
Thoreau, Henry David, 45–46
Tibet, 34–35
Tibetan Book of Living and Dying, The
    (Rinpoche, Sogyal), 188
To Shine One Corner of the World
    (Suzuki), 41–42
Totality and Infinity (Levinas), 89
traditionalism, 109–10
transparency, 11–12, 31–32, 81, 133,
    189, 198
  alonetime and, 183
  vs. darkness, 105
Transparent Self, The (Jouard), 81,
    114–15, 170–71
trauma, 120–22
Trauma of Everyday Life, The (Epstein),
    12–14, 118

travelling lightly, 61–79
  in comfortable "psychological
    clothes," 66–72
  uncovering styles of defense and, 72–79
Trump, Donald, 26–30
Tsung Tsai, 59–60
Tutu, Desmond, 10–11, 37–38, 49
Twain, Mark, 128–29

uniqueness, 12, 14, 198
  humility and, 44
  sense of self and, 100–3
unlearning, 43, 44–45, 72, 183, 198
  Dalai Lama on, 37
  enhancing a spirit of, 45–52
unrecognizable you, exploring, 89–97
Untermeyer, Louis, 80

Vanier, Jean, 162
Vow of Conversation, A (Merton), 15, 164
vulnerability, 28–29, 43

Waddell, Chrysogonus, 71–72
Walls, Laura Dassow, 45
war, 63
Washington Post, 28–29
Washington Square (James), 99
Way of the Dreamcatcher, The (Georgiou),
  70–71, 102–3, 145–46

Way of the Heart (Nouwen), 164
Wehner, Peter, 27–28
Weiss, Andrew, 181, 182
When Things Fall Apart
  (Chödrön), 134–36
Whitman, Walt, 53
wholeness, 30–31
Wiesel, Elie, 161–62
Wilding, Eloise, 205n14
Winnicott, Donald, 177
wisdom, 9, 36–37, 57
wisdom literature, 7–8
Wisdom of the Desert (Merton), 174
Wise Heart, The (Kornfield), 179
Woman in the Polar Night (Ritter), 176
Wooden Bowl, The (Strand), 55–56,
  173
Woolf, Virginia, 85
World War II, 63, 77–79
Writing Alone and with Others
  (Schneider), 15, 150–51

You Play the Girl (Chocano), 33

Zazen, 41–42, 156, 171
Zen Buddhism, 40. See also Suzuki,
  Shunryu
Zen Therapy (Brazier), 112–13, 139–40
Zusya, Rabbi, 8